THE SHENANDOAH VALLEY,
1861–1865

THE SHENANDOAH VALLEY, 1861–1865

The Destruction of the
Granary of the Confederacy

MICHAEL G. MAHON

STACKPOLE
BOOKS

Copyright © 1999 by Stackpole Books

Published by
STACKPOLE BOOKS
5067 Ritter Road
Mechanicsburg, PA 17055
www.stackpolebooks.com

Printed in the United States of America

10 9 8 7 6 5 4 3 2 1

FIRST EDITION

Library of Congress Cataloging-in-Publication Data
Mahon, Michael G.
      The Shenandoah Valley, 1861–1865: the destruction of the granary of the Confederacy / Michael G. Mahon.—1st ed.
         p.   cm.
      Includes bibliographical references and index.
      ISBN 0-8117-1540-X
      1. Shenandoah River Valley (Va. and W. Va.)—History—Civil War, 1861–1865. 2. Shenandoah River Valley (Va. and W. Va.)—History—Civil War, 1861–1865—Social aspects. 3. United States—History—Civil War, 1861–1865—Social aspects. 4. Shenandoah River Valley (Va. and W. Va.)—History—Civil War, 1861–1865 Personal narratives. 3. United States—History—Civil War, 1861–1865 Personal narratives. I. Title.
E470.3.M24 1999
975.5'903—dc21
                                                  99-41087
                                                  CIP

For my mother
Alice May Mahon
and
to the memory of my father
Lawrence Edward Mahon

CONTENTS

ACKNOWLEDGMENTS

As every student of history knows, no author produces a book by himself. During the course of writing this study, a number of individuals provided valuable assistance. Their efforts have made this book better, and for that I would like to extend my sincerest thanks and gratitude.

First, I would like to thank the staffs of the libraries and historical societies listed in the bibliography. In every instance they responded to my many requests for materials with professionalism and understanding. In particular, I would like to thank Patricia Webb of Duke University. Her knowledge of the vast holdings in special collections is surpassed only by her kindness. I also owe a special debt of gratitude to Margaret Cook of The College of William and Mary, who went out of her way to provide me with a copy of the Laura Lee diary. Others I would like to give special thanks to are: John A. Cuthbert of West Virginia University, Rebecca Ebert of The Handley Library, and Christina Bolgiano of James Madison University.

At Stackpole Books, I would like to thank my editor, Michelle Simmons, who worked with me throughout this project. Her comments, suggestions, experience, and skill as an editor have served to make this book better, and I will always appreciate her help for doing so. I further want to thank William C. Davis for his advice and counsel. His suggestion that I examine more closely Sheridan's 1864 Valley campaign proved invaluable, and I will always be in his debt for it. I also would like to thank copy editor Joyce Bertsch, whose efforts made a marked improvement in the text.

Two others that I would like to thank are Randy Rodgers and John Anderson. Although I am certain that they grew tired of hearing about the Shenandoah Valley, they never wavered in their support of doing whatever I asked while working on this project. More important, they are the rarest of individuals: true friends.

Last and foremost, I would like to thank my parents, Alice and Lawrence Mahon, for being who they are, for all their love and support, and to whom this book is appropriately dedicated.

INTRODUCTION

The Shenandoah Valley of Virginia was a critical region during the American Civil War. It was the scene of numerous battles, including two of the war's most spectacular and brilliant campaigns, and as it was a very fertile area, it was often looked to for subsistence.

However, the war had a devastating impact on the Valley's resources and the lives of its inhabitants, who often described in vivid detail in their letters and diaries the pain and hardship they endured. Although initially opposed to the idea of secession, once Virginia did so, the overwhelming majority of the populace openly embraced the Confederate cause and did what they could to support it. But the war continued to demand an ever higher price, which few individuals were able or willing to meet, and within a short period of time, the primary concern of average citizens became the well-being of their familes, though they remained loyal to the Confederate cause. As the war dragged on, the ceaseless demands of the Confederacy led to a growing indifference on the part of the people, and many began to view their own government as just as much an enemy as the Federals. By the end of the war, many Valley residents, though disheartened over the Confederate defeat, were simply relieved that the fighting was over and looked forward once again to working their land and living their lives in peace.

Because of the Valley's agricultural richness, many historians have believed that it was one of the principal sources of supply for the Confederate forces operating in Virginia, some even calling it the granary of the Confederacy. However, by describing the region as such, historians have greatly overestimated the importance of the Shenandoah Valley as a source of subsistence. Contrary to popular belief, the Valley was not a major source of supply for the Confederacy during the war. By the fall of 1862, its vast resources had been depleted. The supplies obtained from the region that year were far less than half of what they had been the year before. Thereafter, the small quantities found in the Valley were used largely to support the troops stationed in defense of the region. Sheridan's destruction of the Valley in 1864, colorful and dramatic as it was, did not deprive the Confederacy of any measurable amount of subsistence or help hasten the fall of Richmond.

The misrepresentation of the Valley's importance as a food source is in large part because scholars have relied on Federal records to substantiate their claims. This study, on the other hand, examines the issue from the Confederate stand-point, and is based on the records and correspondence of the Subsistence, Quartermaster, and War Departments; the dispatches of Robert E. Lee and his subordinates; the diaries and letters of local civilians; and recently discovered tax-in-kind records and other materials. Based on this evidence, this book demonstrates that the Shenandoah Valley was not the granary that historians have alleged.

CHAPTER 1

"The Daughter of the Stars"
History of the Valley

The Shenandoah Valley of Virginia has long been recognized as one of the most beautiful regions of the United States. Flanked on the west by the Allegheny Mountains and on the east by the Blue Ridge Mountains, the Valley runs southwestward for more than 165 miles to the James River, south of Lexington, Virginia. It ranges in width from 20 to 40 miles and can easily be reached from the east or west through the many passes and gaps that cut through both mountain ranges.[1]

In early times, the Valley was primarily a vast prairie of bluegrass and clover. Forests and dense stands of timber were found only along the banks of rivers and streams and in the mountain hollows. Buffalo, deer, elk, bears, wolves, beavers, and other wildlife roamed the low, rolling countryside.

Before the arrival of Europeans, the Valley was the domain of the Cinela, Susquehanough, Senedo, and Tuscarora tribes, which resided along the rivers and streams. Catawbas, Cherokees, Shawnees, and Delawares, who lived in neighboring regions, often visited the Valley.[2]

Every year bands of young braves stalked the migrating herds up and down the Valley, always mindful to take only what they needed, thus assuring an ample supply for the future. The Indians routinely set fire to the dry grasses every fall, preventing the forests and thick underbrush from overtaking the open prairie and ensuring that fresh grass would be plentiful in the spring. The richness and fertility of the Valley awed the Indians; believing that it was a gift from the heavens, they named it the "Daughter of the Stars."

Virginia governor Alexander Spotswood is generally recognized as the first non-native to discover the Valley. On September 5, 1716, with about thirty horsemen, he ascended the Blue Ridge Mountains and gazed upon the broad open vistas of the Valley below. Descending the western slope of the mountain, the men traveled for several miles until they reached the Shenandoah River, where they camped for the night. Upon their return, Spotswood and his men gave radiant accounts of the newly discovered Valley, describing it as a region teaming with wildlife, its sparkling rivers and streams packed with fish and the forests covered with verdant flora.[3]

Nevertheless, most Virginians remained reluctant to move west of the Blue Ridge. Determined to populate the region, the colonial government hired professional agents to attract settlers. These agents found large numbers of colonists in Pennsylvania and Maryland who were more than willing to cross over the Potomac and begin a new life. The overwhelming majority of these people were Germans and Scottish-Irish—proud, religious, industrious, hard-working individuals, with a folk culture that was quite different from that of the Virginians of the eastern plain. They came in search of religious freedom and the cheap, fertile land found in abundance in the Valley. The Germans came to occupy most of the northern half of the Valley, and the Scottish-Irish populated the southern portion of the Valley, which came to be known as the "Irish Tract."[4]

Although the Germans and Scottish-Irish had come to dominate the Valley, it was not theirs exclusively. The prime land also attracted a significant number of Dutch pioneers, and some small groups of English settlers also moved to the Valley. In time, the population became somewhat more diverse, as pioneers of several other nationalities arrived.[5]

By the beginning of the nineteenth century, the Valley still had the look and feel of the frontier, and it would take another decade or so before the vibrant economy developed, but an economic and social infrastructure was evolving that would eventually enable it to become one of the most prosperous sections of the state. Another factor that contributed to its prosperity was the continued growth of the numerous towns and cities that had been founded throughout the valley during the previous half century. Soon after building homesteads in a particular area, residents would petition the Colonial Assembly to pass an act authorizing them to establish a town in the country where they resided. Extremely small at first, usually with only a courthouse, church, general store, blacksmith shop, a few private residences, and possibly a tavern, these towns functioned primarily as places for people to congregate and discuss the events and problems of everyday life. On special occasions, such as a holiday or a county fair, the streets would be jammed with the county's inhabitants taking part in the festivities.[6]

In the succeeding decades, however, as thousands of new settlers migrated to the region, these towns developed more and more into commercial centers. Skilled craftsmen replaced the general store owner, and by the middle of the nineteenth century, shops specializing in the manufacture of shoes, men's and women's clothing, leather goods, hats, furniture, wagons, lumber, and other products lined the streets and avenues of the cities and towns throughout the Valley.[7]

Winchester, founded in 1743, was the first city in the Valley, and by the end of the eighteenth century, the inhabitants of the region had established more than a dozen other towns and cities as well. To the north of Winchester were the cities of Charlestown, Martinsburg, Shepherdstown, and Harpers Ferry. A short distance south of Winchester were the communities of Woodstock, Mount Jackson, Front Royal, and Edinburg, and in the southern section of the Valley were the towns of Lexington, Staunton, Port Republic, and Harrisonburg. By 1860, over 22 percent of the Valley's inhabitants resided in these small urban centers.[8]

The cities improved steadily throughout the early 1800s, and by the 1850s they were flourishing. The most prosperous town in the southern portion of the Valley was Staunton, founded in 1761. Located in one of the richest agricultural regions of the state, and having both road and railway connections with northern Virginia and the eastern plain, the town rapidly developed into the leading transportation hub for the southern Valley.[9]

But this had not always been the case. Until well after the Revolution, the region suffered from a shortage of dependable roads, especially in the southernmost parts of the Valley. Winchester was the principal export town during the early years of settlement, and farmers shipped their products to market via the Shenandoah River and its tributaries. Barges laden with wheat, corn, and raw materials floated down the Shenandoah to Winchester, where their contents were transferred to wagons for shipment to Baltimore, Philadelphia, Washington, D.C., and other nearby destinations. In the Valley, the Shenandoah River and its tributaries flow northward toward the Potomac. Thus, to go downstream is to go northward, while to go upstream is to go southward. As a result, in a lexicon unique to the region and still in use today, the northern portion of the Valley came to be known as the Lower Valley, and southern portion as the Upper Valley.[10]

Eventually, the farmers' burgeoning harvest outpaced the capabilities of water transport and accelerated the need for an extensive road system, and by 1830, a vast network of roads cut through the local countryside. A paved turnpike from Winchester to Staunton, the forerunner of the modern highway, was completed in 1840. Construction of the Pike, as the road came to be known by local inhabitants, stimulated the development of a number of other highways over the next decade, radiating from Winchester to Berryville, Millwood, and Front Royal.[11]

During the next two decades, the Valley, like the rest of the country, was involved in the expansion of the nation's railroads. The first to link up with the Valley was the Baltimore and Ohio, by far the largest railroad operation in the region. Extending its way across the low, gentle countryside of eastern Maryland, the line crossed over the Potomac at Harpers Ferry and pushed on through the Lower Valley. After entering Martinsburg, the line swerved until it reached the Potomac, where it turned west and continued on to the Ohio Valley.

The railroad had a profound impact on the development of the Lower Valley. Almost overnight, Martinsburg and Harpers Ferry emerged as major communication and transportation centers, and realizing what the railroad would mean to its future prosperity, civic leaders in Winchester quickly built a connecting line to Harpers Ferry to link up with the Baltimore and Ohio. Goods and agricultural products from as far away as southwest Virginia and Tennessee made their way to the thriving depots and warehouses of these towns for shipment, and the proprietors of these establishments became some of the wealthiest businessmen in the Valley.[12]

Increased demands for better access to distant markets led to the construction of two more rail lines in the decade before the Civil War. Surveyed and built during the 1850s, the Manassas Gap Railroad provided farmers and merchants in the central part of the Valley with a convenient and economical way to export their products. Designed to unite with the Orange and Alexandria Railroad east of the Blue Ridge Mountains, the line originated at Manassas Junction, 25 miles southwest of Washington, and traveled west across the Piedmont section of Virginia. Traversing the Blue Ridge at Manassas Gap, the line bridged the Shenandoah River at Front Royal and continued on to Strasburg. From there, the track ran south to its terminus at Mount Jackson. When completed, the railway afforded express service to Alexandria, Gordonsville, Richmond, Washington, D.C., and a number of other localities east of the mountains.[13]

In the Upper Valley, the towns of Harrisonburg, Lexington, and Staunton had access to the Virginia Central Railroad. First running north and then west from Richmond, the line made its way through Gordonsville and Charlottesville before crossing over the Blue Ridge via Rockfish Gap. The line next passed through Staunton, then curved to the southwest until it reached Covington, at the base of the Allegheny Mountains. The state considered a plan to extend the track west to the Ohio River, but the outbreak of the war prevented its implementation.[14]

The comprehensive road and rail networks were significant factors in the economic growth of the Valley, because they gave local farmers a distinct advantage over those in other parts of the state. They were able to ship their products to local and distant markets more quickly and efficiently, giving them added incentive to increase production. This they did, and the farmers were rewarded for their hard work and long hours in the fields with yields that were among the highest in the state.

By 1820 the production of corn, oats, rye, barley, and especially wheat had blossomed into major enterprises. Making use of the latest technological advances—fertilizers and the iron plow—Valley farmers in the 1830s obtained wheat yields more than double the state average. The region, which contained eight of the top ten wheat producing countries in the state, so dominated in the cultivation of wheat that in 1850 it produced 28 percent of the state's total harvest. At this time, farmers in the Valley also enjoyed a standard of living that was twice as high as that of other parts of the state. Between 1850 and 1860 a number of landowners saw the cash value of their farms increase by more than 35 percent. In the years prior to the Civil War, Shenandoah Valley farmers were annually exporting over a million and a half bushels of wheat to outside markets.[15]

One of the factors behind this success was the inventive spirit of Valley native Cyrus McCormick, the son of a Rockbridge County farmer. Envisioning a better way, this enterprising twenty-two-year-old in 1831 invented a machine that came to be known as the Virginia reaper, which could cut up to 2 acres an hour. It eventually gained widespread use and transformed agricultural production throughout the United States.

The farmers of the Valley did not limit themselves to the cultivation of grains. They also grew a wide variety of fruits and vegetables and excelled in the raising of livestock. Some of the finest cattle in America grazed in the lush pastures, and by the 1850s, the Upper Valley was acknowledged as one of the foremost livestock-producing regions of the state. The farmers' animals also provided ample dairy products, as well as large quantities of manure, which was used to enrich the fields before planting.[16]

Although Virginia would one day risk everything it owned, with tens of thousands of its brave young men sacrificing their lives in defense of states' rights concerning the issue of slavery, Shenandoah residents overwhelmingly rejected the institution. In 1850, slaves constituted only 20 percent of the Valley's total population, and this declined to less than 18 percent by the time of the Civil War. Nearly every religious denomination in the Valley opposed the concept of slavery, and ministers continually preached to their congregations about its evils and that it was against Christian beliefs to hold another human being in bondage. Moreover, the employment of slaves was largely unnecessary here, as Valley farmers cultivated grains as their cash crops rather than tobacco, which was much more labor intensive. The farms here were generally small, and most farmers worked their land with the aid of their families; if they did require additional hands, generally during times of planting and harvesting, they hired temporary laborers or called upon their neighbors for assistance.[17]

In many ways, the Valley had more in common with its northern neighbors than with the rest of Virginia. Between the Blue Ridge and the Alleghenies, the two great staple crops that had come to symbolize the South, cotton and tobacco, were virtually nonexistent. Valley farmers shipped their products, chiefly wheat and rye, to the constantly expanding markets of the Northeast, not the South. Social relationships reinforced this bond even further, as families stayed in close contact with Northern relatives after moving south of the Potomac. Politically, the residents' views on many issues mirrored those of the North. This was especially true in regard to secession. Shenandoah residents vehemently maintained that the Southern states could best defend their constitutional rights by remaining in the Union, and they rejected any notion of forming a Southern Confederacy. Yet in spite of their differences, the people were proud to be Virginians, and no one ever questioned their loyalty or devotion to the state.[18]

In the politically charged climate of the time, John Brown's raid on Harpers Ferry in October 1859 reaffirmed the Valley's affinity with the Deep South, as it stirred the passions of the nation, with the North looking upon Brown as a saintly martyr sent by God to smite an evil institution that was tearing the country asunder, while the South viewed him as an instrument of the devil intent upon destroying the very foundation of Southern society. Galvanized by Brown's actions, the South demanded the adoption of a slave code, which the North refused to accept. Valley citizens agonized over the turn of events and the ominous direction they were taking. Many surely understood that if this disagreement over slavery was not resolved soon, blood would be shed, and that much of this blood would be theirs, as the Valley, so productive in times of peace, would be coveted even more during wartime. As the crisis deepened, everyone looked anxiously to Washington, but the qualities necessary to defuse the crisis—wisdom, moral courage, understanding, and a willingness to compromise—were lacking in the political leaders of the day. The country would long suffer because of their shortcomings.

CHAPTER 2

"The Most Painful Vote I Ever Gave"

Prelude to the Civil War

As the election year of 1860 began, the nation remained riveted on the seemingly never-ending sectional crisis. And while practically everyone agreed on the seriousness of the situation, few truly believed the Union would dissolve because of it. In the Valley, the *Staunton Spectator* professed surprise that there were any serious apprehensions about the stability of the Union. "With the exception of the insignificant faction of the ultra abolitionists at the North and a few equally insane gentlemen of the fire-eating stripe at the South, nobody seems disposed at present to tolerate the idea of a dissolution. On the contrary the preeminent men of all the great parties, of both sections of the Confederacy, are bold in the declaration that the 'Union must and shall be preserved.'" Initial events seemed to bear this out. In Virginia, the furor caused by the John Brown raid began to subside soon after his trial and subsequent execution in early December, and by the start of the new year, the political leaders directed their attention to more pressing party matters.[1]

Events at the National Democratic Convention in Charleston, South Carolina, however, showed that the threat of secession was very real. It was clear from the start that most Southerners had come to the convention with one objective in mind: to deny Illinois senator Stephen A. Douglas the nomination. Toward this end, a number of delegates from the Deep South, prompted by William Lowndes Yancey, a fire-eating secessionist from Alabama, insisted that a Federal slave code plank be incorporated into the Democratic platform that would protect the institution from any form governmental interference. When the convention voted against this plank, the delegations from Arkansas, Texas, Florida, Georgia, Louisiana, Mississippi, Alabama, and

South Carolina announced their withdrawal and, led by Yancey, walked out of the convention.

The Republicans, on the other hand, found themselves in a much more advantageous position when they assembled for their national convention in Chicago on May 16. Lincoln, their leading candidate, vehemently opposed the institution of slavery, but realizing the consequences, he did not advocate that drastic measures be implemented against it, and he had managed to retain his reputation as a moderate despite his well-known "house divided" speech.[2]

If the secessionists were hoping to find the populace of the Shenandoah Valley sympathetic to their cause, they were sadly mistaken. When confronted with the choice of union or disunion, the overwhelming majority of its citizens unequivocally chose the former.

From his residence in Harrisonburg, in the heart of the Shenandoah Valley, C. C. Strayer, one of the town's more prominent citizens, kept abreast of the events transpiring at the Democratic National Convention in Charleston. He scoured the papers for information of each day's activities, read the speeches of the major participants, and asked his friends for any news they might have heard. Leading up to the convention, Strayer's attitude toward the current crisis was one of guarded optimism, but after its adjournment, his outlook changed to one of despair and anger. Writing to his close friend, John T. Harris, representative of the Ninth Congressional District, he wondered what would become of the party in light of the Southern walkout, what would happen if all of the Southern states bolted the convention, and declared that "if Virginia secedes I am afraid we are gone." A week later, he wrote:

> The Southern democracy have acted in bad faith towards their Northern brethren. For no matter what differences of condition was put upon the Cincinnati platform in the Convention of 1856, as to the power of the people of the territories, there was no difference as to the power of Congress over the subject. We all agreed, North & South, that Congress should not interfere or *intervene*. Now we of the South are contending that Congress shall intervene to protect slavery in the territories. This is a departure from *principle*; and although I think all kinds of property should be adequately protected, yet the Democratic party south would be guilty of dishonor to insist now upon Congressional intervention. I believe that abandonment of the doctrine of the Cincinnati platform will end in the overthrow of the party—and the dissolution of the Union.[3]

Throughout the summer and fall, numerous Union meetings and rallies were staged where hundreds, sometimes thousands, of the Valley's residents gathered to hear local community and political leaders—Alexander H. H. Stuart, John B. Baldwin, Andrew H. Kennedy, and Congressmen Waitman T. Willey and Alexander R. Boteler—denounce the idea of secession as a way of solving the country's ills.[4]

The newspapers also rejected secession as an acceptable alternative. From the opening of the campaign up until the day of election, the Valley's papers called on their readers to stand firm in their dedication to the Union. An editorial in the *Lexington Gazette* asserted that a dissolution of the Union "would be a calamity to all. But to none would the consequences be more serious than to Virginia. . . . The State of Virginia will become the perfect slaughter pen. Every hill and valley will be reddened with human gore. . . . Disunion can be no remedy. So far from it, it will make the very evils worse, for the redress of which, it is pretended." The *Staunton Spectator* stated that when the American people believed that the "Union was really in peril, they would rise in their majesty and their strength to rebuke the traitorous designs of corrupt and selfish men." Two weeks before the election the paper again reminded its readers that "the great and important issue is union or disunion. Will we remain a united, free prosperous and happy people, or shall we be involved in all the evils of anarchy and discord, and all the indescribable horrors of civil war and fratricidal strife?" In the northernmost part of the Valley, the *Charlestown Virginia Free Press* chided the Southern radicals for bringing about the crisis and then asking the Democratic Party to come to their rescue when they realized that their candidate had no chance of success. A week before the voters went to the polls the paper reminded them to not "give the slightest heed to the ranting of the Disunionists. . . . We repeat, let the true friends of the Union stand firm to their cause and their candidates. . . . We need no smooth-tongued babblers from other regions to come and tell us how much we are aggrieved. We can take care of our own honor, and defend our own rights when improperly assailed."[5]

Lincoln ran away with the national contest, as expected, and although they were disheartened by the magnitude of the Republican victory, Lincoln's election did little to change the attitude of the Valley's residents, who were predominantly Democratic, toward secession. In the Upper Valley, the people held mass meetings where they pledged their loyalty to the Union and decried any attempt to bring about its disruption. The *Staunton Spectator* even went so far as to equate secession with treason: "It remedies no wrongs, relieves no evils, redresses no grievances. . . . It has neither of the virtues, wisdom, bravery,

Levi Pitman. A native of Mount Olive in Shenandoah County, Pitman was one of a handful of Valley residents who voted for Abraham Lincoln in the presidential election of 1860. Resented by most of his neighbors because of his political leanings, Pitman nevertheless was tolerated because of his talents as an artisan and craftsman.

nor patriotism, but is foolish, cowardly and treasonable." At a public gathering in Shenandoah County, the citizens called for a convention of the slave states so they could consult and formulate some kind of plan to extract concessions from the North and thus preserve the Union.

Assessing the public's state of mind in Lexington, James B. Dorman informed Governor Letcher that "the people here are thoroughly Union in feeling. They will not follow the lead of South Carolina, but will struggle honestly and with determined purpose for the continuance of the confederacy." Another Lexington resident who adamantly believed in the preservation of the Union was George Junkin, president of Washington College. "We are in fearful times," he declared to a close friend. "I feel like Gen. Jackson—the Union must and shall be preserved—and 'Their object is disunion, but be not deceived, disunion, by armed force, is *treason*.' I hope no one will be hung, tho' a few deserve it."[6]

The inhabitants of the Shenandoah did not consider Lincoln's election sufficient reason to leave the Union. The Harrisonburg *Valley Democrat* maintained that the "idea that a state has the legal right to withdraw from the Union, without the violation of the Constitution, is absurd, and would make our government the most unstable in the world, and convict the framers of the Constitution of weakness and inability to remedy the evils of the old confederation." The *Lexington Gazette* drew a similar conclusion. "If the election of one candidate over another is sufficient cause for a dissolution of the Union, then its existence, with as good reason, might have been endangered at every election that has taken place."

Even John D. Imboden from Augusta County, viewed by most as an avid disunionist who wanted nothing more than for the South to leave the Union, agreed that a legitimate grievance had not yet arisen to warrant such action. Writing to his political confidant, John H. McCue, in neighboring Albermarle County, Imboden stated "that the entire South will speedily have to leave the Confederacy under the present Constitution I entertain no doubt whatever— but I don't think S.C. has put the issue upon defensible ground. . . . To break up the Government for the mere loss of an election is not regarded by thousands as justifiable. It is a mere pretext on the part of disunionists per se to precipitate a revolution." To Imboden, it would be better for the South to await an actual violation of their rights before seceding; then they would be united in their course of action.[7]

South Carolina, however, had no intention of waiting. Immediately following Lincoln's election, the South Carolina legislature called a special convention, and on December 20, 1860, amid much fanfare and ceremony, adopted an ordinance of secession. This dramatically intensified an already volatile situation. Disunion had now become a reality.

In Virginia, Governor Letcher responded to the disruption of the Union by calling the legislature into special session. A political moderate, Letcher had not given up all hope of preserving the Union when he addressed the legislature on January 7, 1861, though recent events had tempered his outlook considerably. "It is monstrous," he said, "to see a Government like ours destroyed merely because men cannot agree about a domestic institution." In a last-ditch effort to avert what would surely be a national catastrophe, he called for a convention of all the states to see if a settlement could be reached that was amicable to all parties. Letcher also made it clear that Virginia would oppose the use of coercion by the Federal government as a means of keeping the Union together. He opposed holding a state convention, at least for the time being. The legislature agreed with Letcher on the use of force, but after a heated debate, it passed a bill that called for a state convention on February 13 to determine what course Virginia should take regarding secession. It also called for an election on February 4 in which the voters would choose delegates to the convention and decide whether the actions taken by the convention had to be ratified by the people.[8]

The legislature's decision to have a convention did not come as a surprise, since calls for one had been raised throughout the state for weeks. Still, many of the Valley residents opposed the idea. In their view, the current circumstances did not require one, and it would only be used by the secessionists to try to persuade Virginia to leave the Union. But to ensure the preservation of their rights and liberties, and prevent Virginia from leaving the Union without their consent, numerous Valley papers and community leaders urged the people to vote for an initiative that would force the convention to submit its actions to them for ratification.[9]

Designed for the purpose of selecting delegates to the convention, the election in a real sense became a referendum on how the people felt toward secession—at least for the moment. In the short but intense campaign that followed, candidates of various political persuasions—from out-and-out secessionists to devoted unionists and everything in between—campaigned hard to win the hearts and minds of voters. With the majority of the Valley's inhabitants still firmly committed to the Union, there was little doubt as to which way the sentiments of their delegates would lean.

Election day came and went, and when it was over, the adherents of secession had sustained a crushing defeat; of the nineteen delegates selected in the

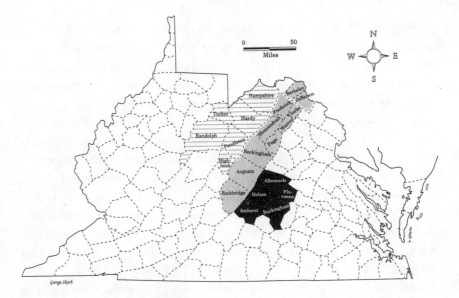

The state of Virginia at the start of the Civil War.

ten Valley counties, only four held that Virginia should secede. The referendum calling for the convention's actions to be approved by the people also passed by a wide margin. Unionists were thrilled with the results. "Lord, how dumbfounded, are the secessionists here!" Valley resident James D. Davidson told his cousin James Dorman, who had just been elected a delegate from Rockbridge County. One individual who reluctantly agreed with this assessment was John Imboden. "I think Va. has turned fool," he angrily declared to a close friend, "but my opinion is contrary to the opinion of the people and I will awate the arbiteament of time to prove who is right."[10]

The majority of Shenandoah residents had once again voiced their opposition to Virginia seceding, but the Unionist victory was not nearly as decisive as it seemed. Although still in the decided minority, secessionists had been making headway in certain parts of the Valley for some time, as evidenced by their partial success in the election. They also proved to be extremely skillful at using recent events—Lincoln's election, the Congressional Republicans' refusal to agree to any sort of compromise, and South Carolina's secession—to arouse the passions of the public and convince them that the South had no other recourse than to secede if they were to protect their rights and property. This line of reasoning influenced many, even some who had previously been the most outspoken critics of secession.[11]

Secessionists also called on Virginia not to turn her back on her fellow Southern states. As the *Winchester Virginian* had declared months earlier, the South was "one family . . . and if South Carolina secedes, and thus inaugurates a final issue with the North, we are necessarily forced to stand in defense of our homes, interests, and people." James J. White of Lexington, an avowed Unionist, stated to a close friend in March that if the "issue is distinctly made, as I imagine, will be the case . . . 'will you go North or South,' my impression is that the people will respond 'Southward,' unless the insane conduct of Southern men should drive them to unconditional embrace of the Union. . . ."[12]

The Valley's residents also made it known that their loyalty to the Union was not without conditions. All attempts by the Federal government to force a state to remain in the Union would be vehemently opposed, and above all else, they wanted their rights and property—by which they meant slaves—Federally protected. On December 31, 1860, Edward S. Kemper of Cross Keys, Rockingham County, wrote to his congressmen that if "every plan that has been offered should fail to secure our rights *in the Union* then it will become Virginians to seek their rights out of the Union." Strasburg citizen C. M. Brown concluded that the North had no intention of giving the Southern people their just rights, and while he hoped they would not force the South "to any rash measures" he was not adverse to using "the point of the Bayonet" to obtain them. Four of Jefferson County's most respected citizens told their congressman, Alexander R. Boteler, that it would be a huge mistake on the part of the Republicans to interpret the results of the recent election as a willingness on the part of Virginia to accept anything less than a just settlement that would guarantee the South all her rights. And in Frederick County, the Reverend B. F. Brooke foresaw the onset of civil war unless the North consented to a change of policy.[13]

The inability of the politicians in Washington and elsewhere to resolve the crisis created an atmosphere of despair, anger, and frustration among many of the Valley's inhabitants. By the end of December, Bolivar Christian, a local state legislator, had become despondent about the ability of the nation to hold itself together. In his opinion, the love and faith that heretofore had served as the bonds of Union had been hopelessly destroyed, and if by some miracle the Union was preserved, it would only be one of convenience. The grounding that previously gave it life, value, and meaning would be gone forever. Moses Walton expressed little hope for the future as well. "If the Republicans," said Walton from his abode in Woodstock, "want to ensure a complete dissolution of the union they have only to preserve in their hostile sentiments such as are contained in the speeches of Wade & others." On the last day of January, Davidson informed Letcher that public sentiment in the Upper Valley was becoming more and more depressed. As for his own feelings, he told the chief executive and his close friend, "whilst I never despair of the Republic, I have forebodings, that there is a determined purpose in the minds of many, to hurry us into conflict, in which our Union will disappear for a time at least, and our peace & lives sacrificed, beyond the power of a generation to repair." In a sermon before the local chapter of the Y.M.C.A., Reverend Brooke preached about the dangers before the Union, yet it seemed to have little effect on many of his subjects: "The older men agreed with me—but the younger generation laughed at my fears. Hot young Blood—eager for war—without knowing what it means."

From the perspective of John Imboden, the country's leaders were deceiving themselves when they talked of saving the Union. "The Union is dissolved," he maintained, "and what's the use to shut our eyes to the fact, if we cannot reconstruct. Lets all go together peacefully if we can, forcibly if we must. For we have but one and the same destiny, one and the same interest. . . . What's the use to deny the true state of the case, and fool & cheat the people by singing hazanahs to the Union when there is no union! I am called a fire eater disunionist . . . but I don't care what they call me. I am going to say what I think and believe, and let the consequences take care of themselves." Virginians everywhere anxiously wondered how Lincoln would respond to the crisis when he was sworn in as president on March 4.

In his inaugural address, the new president assured the Southern states that his administration had no intention of interfering with slavery where it already existed. He furthermore declared to be bound by the Constitution to enforce the fugitive slave laws now in effect, the only question being whether the statutes should be enforced by Federal or state authorities. But he also made it clear that no state could lawfully remove itself from the Union, and said that resolves and ordinances to the effect were legally void. He would, as empowered by the Constitution, faithfully enforce the laws of the Union in all of the states. "In *your* hands, my dissatisfied fellow countrymen, and not in *mine*," Lincoln said, "is the momentous issue of civil war. The government will not assail *you*. You can have no conflict, without yourselves the aggressors."[14]

Reaction to the president's address varied considerably. Corresponding with James Dorman in Richmond, James D. Davidson interpreted the president's comments in a positive light: "I have read the Inaugural, over very carefully. It is about what I expected. Indeed I think it would be unreasonable to expect a Black republican President, to come out decidedly against Coercion in any form. Nor do I think any reasonable Southern man, can draw any inference from it. . . . His avowed determinations, are so much qualified by his *buts* & his *ifs* and his *unlesses* etc, that this inaugural amounts to a message against coercion. I am satisfied his policy is to throw the responsibility of aggression upon the South. . . . The Secessionists here, I do not think, are as much pleased with the inaugural, as they had hoped to be. It is not decided enough for them—it does not smell enough of war and blood. . . . There will be no war, unless amongst ourselves—or brought on by precipitators.[15]

The prevailing sentiments among the Valley's inhabitants toward the president's remarks, however, differed sharply with those of Davidson. Robert Y. Conrad, a delegate to the convention from Frederick County, felt that Lincoln's speech only played into the hands of the secessionists and did absolutely nothing to advance the cause of Virginia remaining in the Union. The *Staunton Vindicator* responded to the address, particularly the comments about the use of force, with hostility and declared that coercion would be *"met by the stern resistance of a united South."*[16]

Robert Young Conrad. A native of Frederick County, Conrad was fifty-six years old when the Civil War erupted. Prior to the war Conrad had attended the military academy at West Point and later resigned from the army to practice law in Winchester. A member of the Virginia Senate from 1840–1844, and during the secession crisis he was elected a delegate to the convention from Frederick County. He died in 1875.

In the wake of the inaugural, secession sentiment gained a new popularity. By the end of March, two of the Valley's leading newspapers, the *Charleston Spirit of Jefferson* and the *Lexington Valley Star,* reversed their positions and announced that the time had come for Virginia to dissociate itself from the present Union. The *Valley Star* claimed that it now advocated Virginia's secession only because it believed all other alternatives had been exhausted. E. C. Burks, of Rockbridge County, a member of the House of Delegates, felt much the same way. In January, he was a moderate in favor of compromise. But in the weeks to come, Burks came to believe the state should make military preparations for its defense. By mid-March, he had given up all hope of an amicable settlement being reached and called for Virginia to sever its ties with the Union. As March came to a close, the *Richmond Inquirer* reported that Shenandoah County had become a firm supporter of disunion and that Rockingham and Augusta Counties also were "coming around."[17]

With the tide of public opinion beginning to turn, those still dedicated to the preservation of the Union clearly understood that the crisis had reached the flash point. A single unintended act on the part of either side would set off a firestorm that would carry Virginia out of the Union and into the arms of the newly formed Southern Confederacy. Representative Harris wrote to an associate: "We are to some extent standing on a volcano which may burst at any moment. One imprudent act at Washington would cause an explosion in our midst which would overwhelm any Union man & plunge the state into disunion. . . . If a strong Southern current once set in, no power on earth can arrest it. When men's heads are once turned to revolution, or distraction, they are past reason." The same thoughts prevailed at the convention. Robert Conrad wrote to his wife that the ongoing struggle between the two sides was a contest of physical strength. In early April, Dorman wrote to Davidson that he feared "business of a civil kind is nearly at an end. In *strict confidence* I have little heart for anything with my apprehensions of what is soon to be upon us.[18]

The imprudent act that Harris feared was soon in coming. Determined to evict the Federal troops occupying Fort Sumter, Confederate shore batteries ringing Charleston Harbor in the early-morning hours of April 12 opened fire. The final outcome was never in doubt, and the garrison surrendered two days later. Lincoln responded to the attack by issuing a call for 75,000 militia to put down an insurrection "too powerful to be suppressed by the ordinary course of judicial proceedings."

Following the Federal call for troops, events in Virginia moved rapidly. Lincoln's decision to use force proved to be the death knell for the coalition of moderates and conservatives trying to keep Virginia in the Union. Virginians would not allow coercion to be used against a fellow Southern state, nor would they furnish military forces to do so. Consequently, on April 17, the secession convention voted 88 to 55 to adopt an ordinance of secession. Virginia was out of the Union, but of the nineteen Valley delegates, only seven voted for the resolution.[19]

Law required that the ordinance be approved by the citizens of Virginia. An election on May 23 would decide the issue, but there was no doubt as to the result. Lexington resident James D. Davidson described to R. M. T. Hunter how quickly public sentiment had changed in his part of the Valley in the aftermath of Lincoln's proclamation: "I gathered around me, in my office some 30 of our strongest Union men and prepared a dispatch to our delegate Dorman in which they all concurred—'Vote an Ordinance of Revolution *at once*.'" In Winchester, James Marshall declared that the citizens were against secession, but if threatened by invasion, they would fight before submitting to Northern aggression. Alexander H. H. Stuart, of Staunton, lamented Virginia's decision to secede and resigned himself to the fact that the people would bow to the will of the convention. "We have been taken out of the Union & into the Southern Confederacy, in the most precipitate manner," he wrote to Waitman T. Willey in a confidential letter. "But what can we do? . . . Our people have not changed their sentiments, but will acquiesce in the action of the convention. . . . I am satisfied that a day of retribution to the conspirators, who have brought the difficulties on the country is not far distant."

The ordinance passed by a large margin both statewide and in all of the Valley counties except Berkeley, where the residents were still unwilling to accept the idea of Virginia leaving the Union and rejected the measure. When forced to choose between the Union and the South, the overwhelming majority of Valley residents ultimately chose the latter, but they did so with the gravest of reservations, and Francis McFarland likely spoke the sentiments of many when he commented after casting his ballot: "This is the most painful vote I ever gave. The course of the Administration, making actual war upon the South to compel them to remain in the Union, or return to it, seemed to leave no alternative. I mourn in bitterness over the state of things, but Va. did all she could for peace.[20]

But vote for secession they did, and in doing so, the residents of the Shenandoah Valley placed themselves in the forefront of a civil war that would shape their lives and destinies to a degree they never could have imagined.

CHAPTER 3

"This Is Only the Beginning, I Fear"

1861

The war that began in Charleston Harbor quickly made its way to the countryside of Shenandoah Valley. On April 18, 1861, four days after the fall of Fort Sumter and one day after the Virginia Legislature had passed the ordinance of secession, Virginia military forces seized the U.S. arsenal at Harpers Ferry, capturing several thousand stands of small arms and valuable arms machinery. Ten days later, Governor Letcher commissioned Thomas J. Jackson colonel of Virginia volunteers, appointed him commander of the forces at Harpers Ferry, and directed him to organize and train the volunteer companies being formed in the Lower Valley. In early May, Jackson received authorization to extend the call for volunteers south to the Valley counties of Page, Warren, Shenandoah, and Rockingham.[1]

These recruiting efforts proved to be extremely successful. At the start of the war, Valley residents exhibited a strong burst of patriotic spirit. Thousands of young men enlisted at the first call to arms; in many areas, hardly a youth under the age of sixteen could be found at home. A week after the capture of Harpers Ferry, approximately 1,300 volunteers had assembled there, and by May 11, more than 4,500 troops were being drilled mercilessly in the hot Virginia sun under the watchful eye of Jackson. This number continued to grow in the weeks and months that followed. In an oft-repeated scene, newly formed companies would meet at their town's courthouse or public square and receive a rousing send-off from local inhabitants, with many a tear shed by family, friends, and loved ones as they marched off to the front.[2]

A variety of factors prompted these young men to enlist, though the primary reason was surely their sense of duty to their state and to the Confederacy. Scribbling a few lines to his family before his unit moved out, Robert Hooke of Harrisonburg made it clear that he did not relish the thought of going off

Reuben A. Scott. A resident of Port Republic, in Rockingham County, Reuben entered the Confederate army in April 1861 as a private, Company B, 10th Virginia Infantry Regiment. Wounded at the Battle of Chancellorsville in May 1863, he was later taken prisoner at Port Republic in September 1864 and was paroled on May 23, 1865. After the war he returned to Port Republic where he lived as a farmer until his death in 1912.

Mary (Mollie) Catherine Saufley Scott. A resident of Port Republic, Mary was in her twenties at the time of the Civil War. Well educated, she attended the Fair View Academy as a young lady. In September 1861 Mary and Reuben got married, while he was on leave, and for the remainder she kept in close contact with him through letters, keeping him apprised of family matters.

to war, but duty and honor obliged him to do so. "It goes right hard," he declared, "for me to leave but I intend to hold to my Company and defend my Country." Reuben Scott also did not cherish the idea of becoming a soldier; in fact, he hated every aspect of it—the constant drilling, the military displays and parades, the harsh living conditions and the lack of food—but he told his fiancée, Mary Saufley, back home in Port Republic, that "at this particular time I think it is my duty to serve my country." Yet many a youth volunteered because of the belief that the war would be a glorious adventure, full of romantic escapades. As a young teenager, Thomas Ashby remembered that most of the boys who signed up from the Front Royal area regarded the war as a "mere outing for pleasure," and never considered the thought of being killed or maimed. In Lexington, Edward Moore recalled that immediately after the firing on Fort Sumter, the youths of the community walked about with huge bowie-knives hanging from their belts because they believed "cold steel" would somehow play a role in the conflict. John Opie, who served in the cavalry under Jeb Stuart, openly acknowledged that he and many of his friends could not think of why they enlisted. In hindsight, though, he admitted that his difficulty with mathematics probably had a lot to do with it.

To those who initially resisted the urge to volunteer, pressure from friends and lovers often became the deciding factor. Scorned, ridiculed, and ostracized by friends and neighbors, and often rebuffed by lovers, many a lad went into the military just to regain acceptance in the community. Martinsburg native David Strother vividly described the treatment afforded to those who did not readily volunteer: "His schoolmates and companions . . . scarce concealed their scorn. His sisters rallied, reproached, and pouted, blushing to acknowledge his ignominy. His Jeanette, lately so tender and loving now refused his hand in the dance, and, passing him with nose in the air, bestowed her smiles and her bouquet upon some gallant rival with belt and buttons. Day after day he saw baskets loaded with sweetmeats, but not for him. . . . There they went— companionship, love, life, glory all sweeping by to Harper's Ferry."[3]

Though a considerable number of the Valley's youth viewed the impending conflict as a romantic lark, their elders knew better. Confronted with the reality of their children possibly being killed or wounded, their protective instincts took over. With three of his older sons already in uniform, David Moore forbade his youngest son to enlist. Unable to join his brothers in the field, Edward occupied his time by drilling militia units in different parts of the county. As a delegate to the convention in Richmond, Robert Conrad could not leave to return to his family in Winchester, but he notified his brother,

Holmes, to remain at home until he arrived. "Take no part before I come," he said. "Your first duty is now to your family—as you are their only protector at home. Write, at once, to recall Powell, and enjoin him also to remain at home until he sees me."[4]

But the lure of fame and glory in most cases had more sway with a young man than his parents' worries, and in the end all the latter could do was voice their concerns about their welfare and ask God to look over them. In the Valley, as all over the nation, many mothers were in a state of mourning over their sons being called away. From Bunker's Hill, William Hooke, in a letter to his son, Robert, said that the women of the area, grieving over the departure of their husbands and sons, blamed Lincoln for the current situation and would solve the crisis right quick if the could only get their hands on him.[5]

But the war also became an innocent diversion for many, the women especially. Ladies from a number of communities throughout the Lower Valley frequently went to Harpers Ferry or Winchester to observe the soldiers as they drilled on the parade grounds. One such lady was Cornelia McDonald, of Winchester, who wrote in her diary that she found the entire experience exhilarating, with the soldiers in their bright, colorful uniforms going through their maneuvers in perfect order, and their military flags emblazoned with state colors fluttering in the wind. When new companies arrived in Winchester, the ladies often lined the streets to cheer and throw handkerchiefs, flowers, and flags to the volunteers as they made their way to camp. Rev. William Brooke, a longtime friend of cavalry commanders Jeb Stuart and Turner Ashby, also made several visits to the troops, and he saw that they would need much training: "Went to see the soldiers drill—they need it much—quite raw—many of them were raised tenderly—hardships await them now."

Aware of just how vulnerable the Lower Valley was to attack by Federal forces, a number of residents called upon the Confederate government to bolster the region's military defenses. In Richmond, on April 27, the convention delegates from the four Lower Valley counties sent a communiqué to Gen. Robert E. Lee, commander of all Virginia military forces, to voice their concern over the apparent lack of military preparedness. They believed that the Federal forces gathering in Pennsylvania just north of the Virginia border would soon cross over the Potomac and invade the northern Valley counties. The Virginia forces had no cannons, and as several artillery companies were already in Winchester ready to receive and use them, they urgently requested that batteries be dispatched without delay. Three days later, Lee received another letter, this time from several of Winchester's leading citizens. Saying that the city and the countryside north of it were entirely defenseless, the city's leaders called upon the military authorities for aid—in particular arms, ammunition, and a number of capable drill officers—and commented that if "devastation and plunder are to form a part . . . of this war, this is certainly an inviting field for it."[6]

The Confederate authorities in Richmond were aware of the value of Harpers Ferry and the Lower Valley and had no intention of abandoning them to the enemy. After examining the situation, Jackson argued that the former Federal armory should be defended at all costs. Its loss, he said, would open the whole northwestern part of the state to the enemy and damage the morale of the troops. In Richmond, on June 3, Lee told Gen. Joseph E. Johnston, who had succeeded Jackson in command at Harpers Ferry when Virginia state forces came under Confederate control, that reinforcements would be sent to aid in its defense because its loss would be depressing to the Southern cause. In a lengthy dispatch to Johnston ten days later, Samuel Cooper, the adjutant general of the Confederate Army, also reiterated the importance of retaining control of Harpers Ferry. The position was vital, said Cooper, because it was "the entrance to the valley of Virginia, the possession of which by the enemy will separate the eastern and western sections of the State from each other, deprive us of the agricultural resources of that fertile region, and bring in its train political consequences which it is well believed you cannot contemplate without painful emotions."[7]

Johnston did not dispute Cooper's arguments for wanting to retain control of Harpers Ferry, but he realized that from a military standpoint the position was untenable. A Federal force crossing over the Potomac at a point above or below the arsenal could easily get behind it, block off all avenues of escape, and capture the entire garrison. To Johnston, the loss of troops would be a greater disaster than the evacuation of a desirable position. Lee acknowledged Johnston's difficult situation and left it to him to determine the appropriate course of action. To eliminate the possibility of capture yet still remain in a position to resist a Federal advance up the Valley, Johnston retired to Winchester, 25 miles south. From there, he thwarted all Federal incursions in the Valley until the middle of July. The Confederate forces in the Valley were then transported by railroad to Manassas, where they participated in the first battle of Bull Run.[8]

Destined to become one of the major battlegrounds of the war, the Shenandoah Valley had thus far been spared from being the scene of any significant conflict; still, the war continued to have ever-increasing effects on the daily lives of its inhabitants. The thought of the war and the innumerable

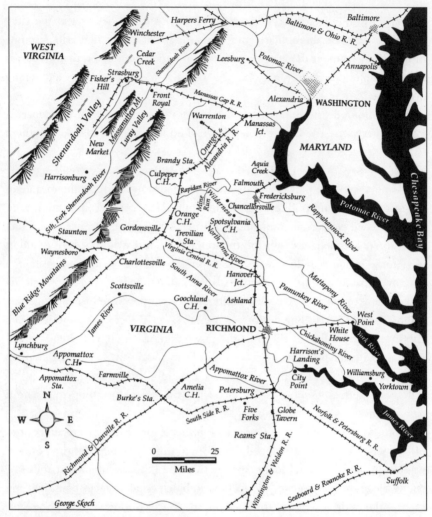

The Shenandoah Valley and the eastern plain of Virginia.

hardships created by it produced a feeling of uncertainty and trepidation among much of the civilian population. Being just a few miles from the frontlines, Winchester's citizens could not help but fear for the future. Julia Chase wrote in her diary: "Into what a sad condition our beloved country has fallen. This will be the worst of wars probably that has ever taken place in the world—and oh what hard fighting there will be."[9]

Still, this did not undermine the desire or willingness of most Valley residents to support the war effort. After the commencement of hostilities, a number of local municipalities raised funds to equip the volunteer companies being raised in the Valley. Ten days after the firing on Fort Sumter, the Augusta County Court appropriated $50,000 to purchase arms and ammunition for the troops and to help support the families of soldiers called into service. A few months later, the Winchester Town Council authorized $10,000 for the same purpose. At a public meeting, the citizens of Rockbridge County passed a number of resolutions calling for the establishment of several different departments to coordinate the collection of money, clothing, subsistence, and new volunteers throughout the county.[10]

Valley residents contributed to the cause in many other ways. Aware of the need for clothing, several congregations in Augusta County got together and made shirts for the troops. With volunteers pouring into Winchester at the start of the war, its residents went out of their way to make sure they received proper food and clothing. Toward the end of summer, newspapers reminded their readers that the winter months would soon be upon them and additional clothing would be needed for the troops. Because woolen goods would soon be in high demand, the *Winchester Republican* called upon residents to increase as rapidly as possible their number of sheep and refrain from eating lamb and mutton. Large quantities of blankets, socks, woolen shirts, shoes, overcoats, tents, and many other articles would soon be needed, and it would take time to acquire them before the onset of winter.[11]

The civilian population, moreover, provided invaluable assistance in tending to the sick and wounded. Because of the rigors of military life, large numbers of young soldiers fell victim to a wide variety of maladies and diseases, the most common being measles, mumps, dysentery, typhoid, and malaria. By early July, the number of sick and wounded in Winchester alone had swelled to more than 2,000. Most public buildings and churches were hastily turned into makeshift hospitals, and as an army medical corps was practically nonexistent at this time, the care of those who became ill depended largely on the generosity of the local residents. Many of Winchester's citizens made repeated visits to the camps and hospitals with supplies for the sick, and when the hospitals overflowed, they willingly opened their homes to give them shelter and care.

Further assistance came from those in other parts of the Valley. With the number of sick in Winchester increasing daily, the *Rockingham Register* issued an appeal to the ladies of the county asking them to furnish whatever articles they could to help alleviate the suffering. A little farther south, Rockbridge native Robert Campbell, over seventy years of age, spent much of his time traveling about the county collecting a wide array of provisions from his fellow neighbors, which he then sent by stagecoach to various hospitals for the convalescing soldiers. In Lexington, many of the ladies routinely accumulated supplies for the sick and wounded and assisted physicians by performing nursing duties. By the fall, these relief efforts became more organized, as residents established soldiers' aid societies within their own communities to assist the military authorities in taking care of the countless numbers of soldiers who succumbed to disease or fell wounded in battle.[12]

The Quakers' antiwar sentiments did not exempt them from the hardships brought on by the conflict. Their meeting houses were soon converted into hospitals for the sick, and many refused to attend services for fear of having their horses and wagons confiscated by the army. "Oh, what a state of things, what a trial we have to bear," Harriet Griffith said in anguish, "and this is only the beginning, I fear."[13]

Although still in its infancy, the war had brought about many changes, one of the most far reaching being the impact it had on the economic vitality of the region. By the spring of 1865, the Shenandoah Valley would be in a state of utter ruin, with homes and farms destroyed, businesses razed to the ground, and the people dazed and disillusioned, but that was still four years hence; in the spring and summer of 1861, good fortune continued to shine on farmers and many business owners, especially those with ties to the military, and they quickly discovered just how prosperous a wartime economy could be. Cut off from their long established markets in the North, the Valley's farmers adapted to the readily changing circumstances by selling their crops to the army, which, with troops pouring into the state from all parts of the South, was more than willing to purchase their entire harvest. As the war progressed, the Confederate government would aggressively seek out and buy all their excess grain and livestock to provide for the military forces operating in Virginia. Many farmers further supplemented their income by hiring out their teams and wagons to the army to assist in the transportation of supplies and equipment.

The conflict also enabled the proprietors of numerous industrial establishments to dramatically increase production—and profits. Skilled craftsmen involved in the manufacture of boots, shoes, wagons, saddles and harnesses, and machinery saw the demand for their goods and services multiply considerably in the weeks and months following the attack on Fort Sumter. Other businesses in the Valley, such as blacksmith shops and iron forges and furnaces, were likewise kept busy with orders from the army to produce or repair military equipment and shoe horses.[14]

With the size of the army increasing daily, the need for clothing became a major concern, and from the moment the war began, the twenty-two woolen mills located in the Valley were operating at full capacity. By the fall of 1861, these mills were producing over 8,000 yards of cloth a day, which laborers converted into shirts, pants, overcoats, and blankets. Harriet Griffith, who worked for her father, Aaron Griffith, owner of Brookland Woolen Mills a few miles east of Winchester, commented in her diary on just how hectic business had become during the early part of July. "We were very busy at the factory, soldiers wanting goods, . . . there was a merchant from Savannah, whom father was anxious to supply, but he had so many others to fill. He would have run two sets of hands night and day if he had them." As with the farmers, when the merchants could no longer ship their wares to the North, they simply redirected their trade to different and more profitable markets. Most of the clothing ultimately went toward satisfying the demands of the military, but a considerable portion also ended up fulfilling the needs of the civilian population, particularly in the ever-expanding city of Richmond.[15]

For those in the Valley fortunate enough to have developed a business relationship with the Confederate government, the war offered an economic opportunity that came along once in a lifetime. Immense profits could be made—one mill owner claimed to be clearing more than $600 a week, which he then promptly sent to Richmond for investment—and if the region had not later been overrun countless times by the military forces from both sides, a much more prosperous and elegant segment of society would have emerged.[16]

But not everyone was able to participate in or enjoy the benefits of this sudden burst of economic activity. With the future uncertain because of the war, many inhabitants refrained from any unnecessary spending. Plans to purchase new clothing, household furnishings, or make improvements on the farm were put on hold, and families made do with what they already had. As a result, a number of businesses that normally would be thriving—men's and women's clothing, furniture, cabinets, plaster, glassware, jewelry, among others—fell on hard times.

It did not take long for the war's debilitating effects to manifest themselves. Declaring that he had never spent a more dreary time in his life as he had since the war began, Lexington resident James Reilly described the local economy as being entirely prostrate by the end of June. Conditions were much the same in Winchester. "Everything is so high . . . and so scarce," lamented a factory worker. "Can hardly be had at all. . . . Business is perfectly stagnant. In the cities nothing else is done but feed and clothe the soldiers."

Even the church could not evade the difficulties brought on by the war. Dependent upon their local communities for financial support, ministers soon found their income reduced as their parishioners were much more reluctant to part with their hard-earned capital. Reverend Brooke took note of his current predicament: "I met with the Church stewards tonight—received $15—Confederate notes—all they could pay on three months' salary. Money comes in slowly and I am in a tight place." Like many of his fellow neighbors, Brooke had no other alternative but to reduce expenses; toward that end he undoubtedly cut back wherever he could, and one of the most painful sacrifices surely must have been his decision to go without tobacco, at least for the month of August.[17]

By the height of the summer, the people would have to contend with a number of other disruptions in their daily lives. Being so close to the front, the threat of attack or invasion by the enemy was always a real possibility. To help augment forces stationed in the Lower Valley, the Confederate authorities issued several calls for the militia to report for duty. These orders did not sit well with the local inhabitants. Husbands did not want to leave their wives and children with the enemy so close at hand. "Men go to the battle field with very little alacrity," wrote Augusta County resident Alexander H. H. Stuart to Secretary of War Leroy P. Walker, "when they feel that they leave their wives and children exposed to horrors to which their own perils are as nothing." Resentful at being called into service, the militia consequently did not exhibit a great deal of enthusiasm. They had little or no respect for their commanders and evaded their responsibilities at every opportunity, opting instead to lounge about Winchester complaining over their plight.

Their lackadaisical attitude did not go unnoticed. Writing to her fiancé, who had answered the first call for volunteers, Mary Saufley, in Port Republic, found it impossible to contain her anger: "I feel greatly provoked to learn how the malitia [sic] have been acting down in Winchester. They are no better than you and many others who have been gone so long. . . . Do they think they are the only ones so situated? Why have they not just as good a right to help defend their homes, liberties, interests and country. They are no better than thousands of others, that have gone willingly three months ago, and in all probability will have to stay much longer than they."[18]

Although people had every right to be outraged by the conduct of the militia, the timing of the draft could not have been worse for the farmers. Called up just as the summer harvest was about to begin, their departure left many a family with no one to work the fields. "The wheat fields will soon be ready for the scythes," said Sarah McKown, of Gerrardstown, "but where are the reapers. . . . It is a sad tale to tell but they have gone to war." With his eldest son already in the army, William Hooke, of Bunker Hill, Augusta County, realized that he would be hard-pressed to work his land if his remaining son, Franklin, had to report for service. But most of the county's young men were being called up, and he held little hope that Franklin would remain at home for long. The suddenness of the draft also prevented many Rockbridge County farmers from harvesting their wheat, oats, corn, and hay, which were said to be the finest crops in years.[19]

By mid-August, the shortage of farm labor had become so acute that the citizens of Shenandoah County petitioned both Governor Letcher and President Jefferson Davis. Citing a scarcity of slave labor, as there were only about 150 adult male slaves in the entire county, the community leaders called upon Letcher and Davis to intercede on their behalf and authorize the release of the county militia so they could return to their homes in time for fall planting. "The labor is performed in a great measure," the petition stated in part, "by those who are in the militia, and if they be continued in service at this critical time, when they should be employed in preparing the land for a fall crop, this vast productive region, instead of being the Egyptian granary whence our armies may be fed in the coming year, will scarcely support our own population."[20]

Anxious to return to their farms, a number of officers from the 7th Brigade, Virginia Militia, sent their own petitions to the governor and the president two weeks later. The men viewed their presence to be largely unnecessary, as more than half of them were still without arms after two months, and the arms provided the others were of the most inferior kind. They believed they could better serve the Confederacy by going home and working their land. "The valley of Virginia is a wheat-growing country, in which slave labor is scarce. . . . The time for seeding the wheat crop has arrived, and unless at least a considerable proportion of the men now here can be returned to their homes to attend to putting that crop in the ground we will be unable to raise supplies sufficient for our own subsistence."[21]

As the war unfolded, Valley residents' horses and wagons were often impressed by the military. Being in close proximity to the troops, residents throughout the Lower Valley often had their horses and wagons drafted for extended periods of time or confiscated altogether. During the winter, farmers raised few objections to the army's use of their teams. There was not a tremendous amount of work to be done on the farm, and they appreciated the extra money the government paid them for their services. During spring planting and summer harvest, however, farmers could ill afford to lend their wagons and work animals to the army. But the soldiers had to be fed, clothed, and supplied with munitions, and when the farmers balked at providing the necessary transportation, the military had no other choice but to impress what they needed. In July army officers informed Rockingham County residents that they would be required to furnish teams to haul provisions for the troops stationed at Laurel Hill, just north of Beverly, and that if they refused, soldiers would be sent to force them to comply. When the army impressed wagons in Rockbridge a short time later, an editorial in the *Lexington Gazette* chastised the officers for not giving the people advance notice. If they had, the paper argued, it would have given the farmers a chance for carrying on their operations, in the proper season. As it was now, many individuals would be unable to get in a full crop at the usual time. One woman complained that several officers went into a field being worked by members of her family and took the horse they were using.[22]

For many, the fear, uncertainty, and anxiety created by the conflict, now an everyday part of their lives, became too much to bear, and rather than subject themselves to continued deprivation and hardship, they packed up and left for more secure surroundings. Within weeks after the capture of Harpers Ferry, much of the civilian population had departed, and by June the town was nearly abandoned. This once quaint and picturesque city, nestled at the base of the Blue Ridge Mountains where the waters of the Shenandoah and Potomac Rivers converge, was now filthy and desolate, with homes abandoned and torn apart for firewood, horsed being stabled in churches, and animals fighting over decaying waste lying in the streets. The harsh living conditions brought out the darker side of the town's remaining inhabitants; men, women, and children could be observed plundering government buildings and private houses at all hours of the day, not the least bit concerned about being seen by their fellow townspeople.

A considerable number of families in Martinsburg, Charlestown, Shepherdstown, and the adjacent countryside also decided that it would be in their best interests to leave. After watching several of his neighbors move away in the weeks following the outbreak of hostilities, one astute individual commented, "The people are beginning to provide for themselves by flight in earnest." Rumors of a Federal invasion had been circulating for weeks, and many were terrified of being left to the mercy and dictate of the enemy. Their departure took on an added sense of urgency when the Confederate forces withdrew from Harpers Ferry in the middle of June and retired to Winchester. The army's withdrawal from Harpers Ferry, in turn, precipitated an exodus from Winchester. Not wanting to be near the front lines, many of its citizens opted to leave rather than stay and be caught in the crossfire when the fighting erupted.[23]

Still, for most Valley residents, leaving was not a possibility simply because they had no other place to go. The predicament of Charles Wesley Andrews, of Shepherdstown, longtime rector of Episcopal Trinity Church, St. Andrews Parish, was probably typical. Andrews, by mid-May, began to wonder how long he would be able to remain in Shepherdstown; if the Federals advanced from Martinsburg as expected, he would have no choice but to leave, a circumstance he hoped to avoid. Being a prudent man, he took the precaution of packing up his sermons and personal effects so as to be able to depart at a moment's notice. Keeping his wife, now in St. Louis with relatives, apprised of his situation, Andrews maintained he was in no personal danger and surmised that if need be he would proceed to Clarke County for a short while and return when the shock of the enemy's actions had subsided. Nevertheless, his assurances that he was safe from harm probably did little to calm his wife's fears, and weeks later he could tell her no more than "where & when I shall go, I know not."[24]

To their credit, the majority of the Valley's inhabitants were a hardy and determined group of individuals. They realized that much of what was happening and what would happen in the future was beyond their control, and that ultimately they had no recourse but to deal with the war as best they could. They reconciled themselves to the fact that the war was now just another, albeit burdensome and unwelcome, part of their daily lives. Amid all the hardships, the McKown family in Gerrardstown continued to work and care for their land as best they knew how, as did Francis McFarland near Bethel Church and the thousands of other farmers living in the Valley. Because of the great scarcity of labor, the farmers assisted one another to ensure the harvest, working in each other's fields until their crops of wheat, corn, oats, and hay were collected and put away in their barns and storehouses.[25]

Even though three months had passed since the bombardment of Fort Sumter, the war in Virginia thus far had been confined to a few minor skirmishes along the border; fighting of a significant nature did not occur until Sunday, July 21, 1861, when the Union and Confederate armies, really little more than armed mobs at this point, clashed at Manassas, a short distance from Washington. The fighting lasted for more than six hours, and when it was over, the Confederates had achieved an overwhelming victory, routing the enemy from the field.

News of the Confederate victory spread quickly, and as expected, it electrified the Southern populace. Former congressman Alexander Boteler's daughter Tippie wrote to her sister from Fountain Rock, the family estate a few miles outside of Shepherdstown, "Such excitement as we all have been in for the past two days you never knew. Extras have been flying and the little news boys screamed like fiends as they yelled and rejoiced over another battle." Francis McFarland, who made a trip to Staunton a few days after the contest, said that there was great excitement about the recent victory, although people were unable to get any particulars about the fighting. Virginia Bedinger, in Lexington, took great satisfaction in recounting the details of the battle in a letter to her mother, who lived in New York. She maintained that the North was merely wasting its time in trying to impose its will upon the South, declaring, "I should think if the people of the North could possibly get at the truth of this battle, it would prove them to utter folly of attempting to conquer the South . . . for our men will fight until the last man is killed, rather than sustain a defeat by such foes."[26]

Within a year, the fight at Manassas would be regarded as little more than a heavy skirmish; at this time, however, the casualty figures shocked and horrified both Northerners and Southerners. In the days immediately following the engagement, families everywhere anxiously awaited word on their loved ones. On hearing of his son's well-being, Marcus Buck, of Front Royal, heaved a sigh of relief and thanked God for watching over him and "turning away the bullets of the enemy." Virginia Bedinger expressed feelings of joy when she heard of her brother's safety: "On Thursday I re'cd a hurried line from him, assuring me of his perfect safety. My heart overflowed with love & thanksgiving to my Heavenly Father for having spared my brother."

But others were not so fortunate. In Lexington, James D. Davidson learned that his son Frederick had been killed and his nephew Preston Davidson seriously wounded. A few days after the battle, Holmes Conrad had to tell his wife the heartbreaking news that their two sons, Holmes, Jr., and Tucker, both had been struck and killed by the same shell, as was their cousin Peyton Harrison. All three had been found lying next to each other on the battlefield. Throughout the Valley, numerous other families had to face the loss of husbands, sons, and brothers. In Martinsburg and Winchester, at least seven other households were in mourning.[27]

The dreadful loss of life awoke the Valley's inhabitants to the harsh reality of war. Up until now, they had mostly been involved in preparation, and though everyone realized that fighting would eventually occur, it had been just an abstract thought in their minds. Never having been involved in a war, most of the Valley residents had yet to fully comprehend the uncompromising brutality inherent in warfare. That all changed after Manassas. "We did not begin to realize the horrors of our victory," said Cornelia McDonald, "till Tuesday evening when the wagons began to come in with their loads of wounded men; some came, too, with the dead." Learning of the gruesome details of the contest, another woman could not but "think of all the sad & stricken hearts throughout the land," and blaming the North, she asked God to forgive her for the deep-rooted feeling of hatred she felt toward the enemy. As a Southerner dedicated to the Confederacy, Tippie Boteler initially viewed the Federal defeat as a cause for celebration, yet she soon felt dismay and horror when she read what the soldiers had experienced during and after the battle.[28]

In Winchester, Julia Chase also expressed shock and disbelief at the carnage. But the thought of the dead and wounded was not the only reason for her feelings of gloom and despair. As one of a small but noticeable number of Unionists still living in the Valley, she was equally disheartened by the outcome of the battle. "Our skies are very dark," she declared. "The Federalists were completely routed . . . at Manassas—& unless God interposes, I fear that this Government will not be able to maintain itself." Yet in spite of her antipathy toward the Southern cause, she still felt for those families that had suffered a loss. "Some hearts will be sad tonight," she said in the aftermath of the fighting, "and though these our townsmen differ from us . . . we feel sad if such should prove true."[29]

Although a decided minority, Unionists could be found throughout the region, though their presence was much more prevalent in the Lower Valley as one traveled northward toward the Potomac. Opposed to secession prior to the conflict, they adamantly remained so after its commencement and made no attempt to conceal their political convictions. "I am more & more against Secess," Reverend Andrews told his wife while performing his duties as rector in Shepherdstown. "It is a monstrous delusion & a monstrous wrong." It did not take long for a sizable Unionist faction to emerge in Winchester, which had the largest percentage of foreign and northern-born citizens in the Valley. These Unionists included middle-class businessmen, merchants, and artisans, as well as Quakers and recent immigrants from the North. Estimates of their numbers range from a low of several dozen early on to several hundred by the time the conflict ended. Many others still loyal to the Federal government could also be found in the countryside west and north of the city.

Unionism, by far the strongest, also manifested itself in considerable portions of Berkeley County and Martinsburg. During the month of May, even though it was obvious by that time that Virginia would secede, those devoted to the Union held a number of mass meetings to demonstrate their support. At one, so many attended that the crowd spilled out of the courthouse and into the street. After adopting a resolution condemning secession and calling on the people to vote against it, they proceeded to select a list of Unionist candidates for the state legislature. One of the county's leading citizens declared the people to be united in their opposition to joining the Confederacy; under no circumstances, he said, would they agree to become a member of it, even if it involved a division of the state. Sentiment against secession was so strong that just before the May 23 election, Jackson considered it necessary to transfer an infantry regiment to Martinsburg to quell threats from Unionists who were doing their utmost to curb "the expression of Southern feeling." Troops already stationed there also were in readiness, as one soldier stated, to put down any riots or disorders if trouble erupted between "the loyal citizens & the traitor mobs" of the town. Passing through Martinsburg several months later, Alexander Barclay, a soldier under Jackson's command, characterized the town as an "abolition hole" that deserved to be burnt to the ground.[30]

Unionism was so pronounced in this portion of the Valley for two main reasons. From the inception of the secession crisis, practically every segment of the populace had long been opposed to the dissolution of the Union. But even more important, in Berkeley County and Martinsburg, unlike Winchester and other sectors of the Valley, many of the most prominent citizens were in the forefront of the resistance movement. One historian who extensively examined the impact the war had upon the civilian population in the Lower Valley estimated that in Martinsburg alone, at least half of the upper class were Unionists. The fact that so many of the county's leading citizens participated in the resistance movement undoubtedly encouraged others, who may otherwise have refrained from voicing their opinion, to come forward.

Of those who remained dedicated to the Union, none was more steadfast than the Pendleton family of Martinsburg. At the time, the patriarch of the family was Philip Clayton Pendleton, a gentleman well in his eighties who, in spite of his age, continued to have significant influence on those around him. His advanced years made it impracticable for him to assume an active role, so it fell to his son, Edmond, to speak for the family. A delegate at the convention in Richmond, Edmond had long opposed secession and refused to sign the ordinance when it passed. Upon his return to Martinsburg, he continued to speak out against secession whenever and wherever the opportunity presented itself. His reputation as an unconditional Unionist became so well known that his friends gave him the moniker of "Edmond, the Staunch and Steady," who, "in the trial of terror and cajolery which subdued so many men of weaker mold," had stood firm in the face of adversity.[31]

The second factor that persuaded many to maintain their allegiance to the Union was the presence of the Baltimore and Ohio Railroad and its impact on the local economy. Making its way across the Lower Valley, the B & O had for decades provided farmers, merchants, and businessmen convenient access to the markets of the Midwest and the Northeast. Equally important, the railroad afforded employment of hundreds of Valley residents, which included a large number of foreign born, Germans in particular, who were staunch Unionists. When the conflict forced the issue and people had to decide whether to give their loyalties to the Confederacy or the railroad, on which their livelihood depended, a large segment unequivocally chose the latter. Although not a Valley resident, a letter writer from Morgan County, just west of Berkeley County, certainly expressed the feelings of many who lived near the railroad when he told a government official a little later in the war: "We belong to Baltimore and live, breathe and have our being on the B. & O. R.R. We want the whole state preserved in its integrity, but if it is to be divided between the U.S. and C.S., we must go with the party that holds the B. & O. R.R. & Baltimore."[32]

The Confederates' decision to destroy the railroad also was instrumental in turning many against the Southern cause. From a military standpoint, the destruction of the railroad was necessary because it would sever the North's most important line of communication and transportation with their forces operating in the west, but from the perspective of the civilian population, the Confederacy was destroying the means on which they depended for their economic survival. The ill will this created did not diminish with the passage of time. Traveling through the region in the fall of 1862, a soldier described the people of Martinsburg as bitter Unionists and maintained that sentiment of a similar nature could be found in every village and hamlet along the B & O railway. Stationed in the Valley at that time, artillery officer Ham Chamberlayne also noticed the evil effects brought on by the railroad. Berkeley County, he said, "is ruined in great part by the B. & O. R.R. . . . That road has caused monstrous harm to Virginia; little along the line is to be seen which can remind one of Virginia as we love to . . . think of her."[33]

Living as they were among Confederate loyalists, Valley Unionists became the objects of scorn, ridicule, and harassment. The contentious atmosphere now so prevalent left Harriet Griffith uncomfortable, and her anxiety only increased when she discovered that members of her family were under constant observation. "Uncle James and Joseph are both watched all the time," she wrote in her diary, "and I fear we are, too. Oh, how careful we must be all the time, and yet we say nothing." The Chase family likewise felt the sting of discrimination.

While most citizens had little difficulty obtaining permission to leave town, Charles Chase found his request quickly denied when he applied for a pass to travel to Martinsburg in August, a circumstance that his daughter attributed to their Unionist affiliation.[34]

For many others, the acts of reprisal went beyond verbal taunts and harassment. In August a Martinsburg store owner had his wares taken from his establishment by Confederate loyalists, who then sold them about town. The following month, A. R. McQuilken, a shopkeeper in Berkeley County, had his stores seized by Confederate cavalry under the command of Turner Ashby. When Ashby asked the authorities in Richmond how he should dispose of the confiscated articles, he was told that they should be regarded as a seizure from the enemy and turned over to the quartermaster and hospital departments in Winchester for distribution. As a member of the Wheeling Convention, McQuilken had the foresight not to remain in town for long, and he quickly fled the Confederacy.[35]

Intimidation and threats of violence played a significant role in subduing many who remained loyal to the Union. This was especially true during the weeks surrounding the election over secession. Reverend Andrews, of Shepherdstown, wrote to his wife that intimidation kept many Unionists from the polls. Examining the returns of the May election, a Charlestown newspaper observed that the final tally in Jefferson County was approximately 600 less than the total cast in the February election. A week after the election, Levi Pitman, visiting a friend in Frederick County, was told not to return to his home in Shenandoah County because several of his neighbors had threatened violence against him due to his refusal to vote for secession. Believing these threats to be real, Pitman remained in Frederick County for more than two weeks, and then contacted friends to make sure it was safe for him to return home.[36]

Then there was the case of William Sperow. A resident of Falling Waters, Berkeley County, Sperow had been a strong Union supporter in the decade before the war. Yet like so many others, he got caught up in the emotional debate over secession, and when the time came, he voted in favor of Virginia seceding. But Sperow almost immediately felt convinced that he had made a terrible mistake, and he openly reaffirmed his allegiance to the Union. His decision to repudiate the Confederate cause and support the Union outraged many of his fellow neighbors. Less than a week after the May 23 election, a group of his neighbors carried off several pieces of his farm machinery. A few days later, while Sperow was in Williamsport on business, an irate citizen struck him from behind with a stick and told him he had less than five minutes to leave town. In the ensuing weeks, Sperow received a number of other threats against his life. Being a cautious man, and fearing for his safety, he left his home several times, returning a short time later when the passion of the moment had subsided. Sperow also had his horses stolen numerous times, as well as saddles, harnesses, and other valuable farm equipment. But Sperow's problems did not end here. Intent on causing him as much trouble as they could, Sperow's enemies managed to get him arrested by the Federals three times on charges that he was spying for the Confederates. The first time he was taken into custody, in July 1861, one of the Federal officers at Harpers Ferry, upon hearing the facts of the case, released Sperow and let him know that all his troubles were directly due to the actions of his neighbors. Sperow was also incarcerated twice during the war by the Confederate authorities and threatened with hanging because of his Unionist leanings.[37]

During the opening months of the conflict, scores, perhaps even hundreds, of other Valley residents were also taken into custody for being opposed to the cause, in many instances on the scantiest of evidence. Wartime diaries and the *Official Records* make it clear that such arrests took place almost daily. In fact, by summer, the number of arrests by the military had grown to the point where Andrew Hunter, of Jefferson County, felt compelled to write to Secretary of War Leroy P. Walker that this practice was actually driving many from the Confederate cause and into the arms of the enemy. To help alleviate the situation, he suggested that a commission be organized, made up in part of loyal citizens, to examine each case individually and dispose of it in the proper manner.[38]

Conversely, the sizable Union presence in the Valley also created problems for the Confederate military forces operating in the region. With a considerable number of citizens hostile to the Confederacy, General Johnston found it increasingly difficult to gather accurate information on the whereabouts of the federal troops. "The enemy's movements cannot be ascertained accurately," he informed his superiors in Richmond in late June. "The population bordering the Potomac in Virginia is all hostile to us; they inform the enemy of every movement of ours, while we know nothing of his but what we see." Former congressman Alexander R. Boteler echoed these sentiments several months later to Secretary of State R. M. T. Hunter, calling upon the government to make General Ashby provost marshal for the counties adjacent to the river. "These counties are infested with traitors," Boteler declared. "They cannot be controlled or guarded against unless some one be invested with the authority to deal with them as they deserve. The defy all authority now, and are in daily communication with the enemy."[39]

It was not only the Confederates who conducted a campaign of intimidation and harassment, however. Following the Confederate withdrawal from Harpers Ferry, the Federals, now in control of a considerable portion of the Lower Valley, began making routine arrests of many prominent citizens who espoused the Southern cause. Often these arrests were in retaliation for the incarceration of loyal citizens by the Confederates. Charles J. Faulkner, one of Martinsburg's foremost residents, was frequently detained by the Federal authorities. Alexander Boteler also faced the prospect of arrest by the Federals. Late in the evening on a hot August night, a detachment of soldiers surrounded the family mansion at Fountain Rock. The officer in charge pounded on the front door, demanding that Boteler come forward so he could be taken into custody. These actions frightened the other members of his family, but what upset them the most was the fact that his arrest was due entirely to the "earnest solicitation of men from *this side of the river.*"[40]

Yet in spite of the animosity, immediate circumstances left the two sides with no other option but to learn to live together. With major portions of the Valley, the Lower Valley in particular, constantly changing hands, it was not in the best interests of either party to antagonize the other too much, because residents never knew when they would need their neighbors' assistance to get by. Helping a neighbor who happened to empathize with the North put in a supply of sugar or salt, or intervening on his behalf when the Confederate authorities came by to question him, usually paid dividends later on when the situation was reversed. Watching this system of tacit mutual cooperation in action, David Strother described how it worked:

> Our fair rebels, meek and plausible, cultivate their Union acquaintances, and through them find means to replenish their empty sugar boxes and flaccid coffee bags, to renew their faded and unfashionable apparel, and to escape the harassing domciliatory visits of the military police. . . . When the ragged rebel rules . . . the starlit banner goes under, and our Union dames nudge their smiling triumphant neighbors, delicately reminding them of former friendships and recent favors, which are not always forgotten. The rebels leave their sick and wounded in the care of the Union man's family, and the bitter memory of wrongs and insults is lost in sympathy for the dying stranger. The disabled Yankee sleeps in security beneath the rebel's roof, and enriches the poor man's scanty board with his varied and superfluous rations.[41]

As bothersome as it was to have a segment of the Valley's populace opposed to the idea of Southern independence, during the opening stages of the conflict, the Confederate government had far more pressing matters to occupy its attention. From the moment hostilities commenced, the authorities in Richmond began to prepare for the expected Federal onslaught, one of the most significant aspects being the accumulation of adequate quantities of subsistence to provide for military forces currently being organized in Virginia.

Having been assigned to the command of the military forces at Harpers Ferry when the war began, Thomas J. Jackson, then colonel of Virginia volunteers, wasted little time in going about the business of furnishing his troops with proper provisions. Finding the commissary department in a deplorable state upon his arrival, Jackson called upon General Lee in Richmond for assistance. "The commissary department here is in a suffering condition," said Jackson, "and will continue so, unless the estimates are complied with. . . . I would respectfully recommend that the money for which estimates have been made by the quartermaster and commissary be turned over to them at once, and, if practicable, that it be deposited in a Winchester or Charlestown bank." Lee responded to Jackson's request by immediately directing the Commissary and Quartermaster Departments to release the necessary funds. At this same time, Lee also notified Jackson that he was on his own in regard to collecting provisions for his troops and left it to his discretion as to how to secure them, the only stipulation being that he was to do as little as possible to interfere with "the legitimate commerce of our citizens." With that objective in mind, Jackson, ever the resourceful commander, while in the vicinity of Martinsburg toward the end of June, began selling the large stockpile of coal at the town's railroad depot to the local inhabitants, using the proceeds to purchase provisions from the surrounding countryside.[42]

In the aftermath of Johnston's decision to withdraw from Harpers Ferry, the War Department in Richmond expressed its concerns, aware of just how vital the Valley was to the Confederacy, both from a military standpoint and as a major source of subsistence. What worried the Confederates most was the increasing attention the enemy seemed to be giving to the region and the possibility that the Federals might attempt to advance up the Valley as far south as Staunton. If that were to occur, they would be able to cut off the Confederacy's ability to communicate with its forces in the west and Deep South, while at the same time be in a position to advance against the forces defending the Confederate capital from the rear. The Federals' task would be made easier by the fact that they would not have to burden themselves with a long supply train; the

Valley itself would be their base and could furnish anything the troops needed. To prevent this from occurring, Cooper directed Johnston to be prepared to resist an invasion and to "strip the county which may be possessed by the enemy of those things which may be most valuable to him, especially horses suited to the military service and herds of beef cattle."[43]

In the weeks and months that followed, the Confederate Military and Commissary Departments continued the never-ending task of accumulating the vast quantities of foodstuffs necessary to support the troops in the field. A major factor behind the Confederacy's success in obtaining subsistence from the Valley was Capt. Wells J. Hawks, who before the war had been a prosperous businessman and one-time mayor of Charlestown, Virginia. When the conflict began, he entered the service with the 2nd Virginia Infantry, from Jefferson County. Having lived in the Valley his entire life, Hawks knew its resources well, and to take advantage of his knowledge, Jackson made him his chief commissary officer, a position he would hold for the remainder of the conflict. Charged with procuring supplies, Hawks wasted no time in putting his talent to work, and although no official documents remain, he did keep a record of what he purchased or impressed. His papers cover most of the war, running from June 1861 to June 1864.

Unfortunately, his records for 1861 are fragmentary and shed no light on the precise quantities of provisions he acquired for the army. But it should also be noted that in the weeks following his appointment, General Johnston, his commander at Harpers Ferry, asked the War Department a number of times to have additional commissary officers appointed to his command so they could properly care for the large quantities of subsistence being collected.[44]

When the army began experiencing supply problems in the weeks following the battle at Manassas, attention turned toward the Valley as a source of food for the troops. Responding to complaints about the lack of subsistence, Secretary of War Leroy P. Walker sent a communiqué to Commissary General Lucius B. Northrop in early September suggesting that the difficulties in supplying the army might be remedied if he had the department obtain additional rations from the Valley. "It is said to be impossible to provide rations ahead for the troops. So it may be if everything comes from Richmond; but if purchases are made in the Valley of Virginia, such as flour, corn, oats, bacon, and beef, it is certainly practicable to accumulate any quantity, as two railroads would be in requisition instead of one." Northrop responded sharply to Walker's recommendation, letting it be known that he did not appreciate the secretary's involving himself in the internal matters of the department, especially when he was not acquainted with all of the facts, and informed him that he already had agents in the region purchasing supplies.[45]

Upon Jackson's return to the Valley in November as commander, he soon became embroiled in a controversy with the Commissary Department over how it conducted business while under his jurisdiction. What aroused Jackson's ire most was the fact that without his knowledge or consent, the department had its own agents in the region offering higher prices for the same items that Hawks and his subordinates were purchasing. This was causing resentment among the farmers who had sold their products at the lower price. Jackson did not want anything to interfere with Hawks's proficiency in gathering supplies for the army. Operating out of Winchester, Hawks on December 9, 1861, notified his superiors:

> I have purchased 1,300 barrels of flour for the army since I have been here. . . . I could get 5,000 bls of flour, in as short a time as it could be sent here. I could if desirable purchase and send to Manassas, a large quantity of flour. The troops at this place cannot consume one third of the flour that can be purchased here. Wagons that bring over our supplies from Strasburg could take back loads of flour for Manassas.

In fact, by December, the railroad lines from the Valley were in such constant use that at times the Virginia Central was limited to the transportation of supplies. By January 1862 over 5 million pounds of rations had been accumulated at Manassas, much of it having come from the Valley.[46]

Situated along the border, residents of the Lower Valley expressed concern about being exposed to the continual ravages of the Northerners. Between late July and the time of Jackson's return in November, the forces under Johnston having been transferred to Manassas, the region had been left to the mercy of the enemy, and Federal cavalry had staged countless forays into the countryside of Berkeley and Jefferson Counties. In early October, Andrew Hunter, of Charlestown, sent a dispatch to Secretary of War J. P. Benjamin to protest the handling of military affairs in this part of the state. Perplexed as to why large bodies of militia were now being quartered in Winchester, 30 miles distant, when they were desperately needed elsewhere, Hunter wrote that the absence of military protection permitted the enemy to launch attacks against the civilian population with impunity and "to debauch the minds of our people off from their allegiance and loyalty to the South."

Jefferson County resident James Ranson was also upset over the enemy's constant transgressions and in mid-October wrote to President Davis: "The enemy crossed over the Potomac at Harper's Ferry last week . . . and have been arriving ever since, pillaging and ravaging as they advanced. The farmers below this place are being robbed of slaves, horses, and everything the enemy can use. . . . The enemy have long been in possession of Harper's Ferry, desecrating our soil, pillaging our defenseless and loyal people, and outraging the sanctity of helpless and loyal families." He went on to say that if military assistance did not soon come, the whole countryside would be devastated, with crops destroyed, mills and factories burned to the ground, and property and slaves confiscated.

Two weeks later, J. H. Sherrard of Winchester also called upon the government to pay more attention to the exposed condition of the border counties. If they failed to do so, he said, the cause of the South would be injured in this part of the state because it would bring about the "withdrawal from it . . . the support of some of the best citizens from the apparent inability of our Government to afford them that protection which they think they have a right to demand." Alexander Boteler also commented on the troublesome circumstances. "The condition of our border is becoming more alarming every day," he told a government official. "No night passes with some infamous outrage upon our loyal citizens."[47]

But contrary to what the Lower Valley inhabitants might have believed, the Confederate government had not abandoned them. The military authorities in Richmond issued orders for Jackson to proceed to Winchester and assume command of the newly created Valley District of the Department of Northern Virginia. Jackson arrived in Winchester on November 4 and immediately began strengthening the Valley's defenses. The next day, he appealed to the secretary of war to have all possible reinforcements sent to him, even if it meant recalling troops from other parts of the state. The same day, the brigade formerly led by Jackson, soon to gain renown as the "Stonewall Brigade," received orders to proceed to the Valley to rejoin their old commander. A short time later, militia units were directed to Charlestown and the surrounding neighborhood. The presence of veteran troops and a capable officer such as Jackson helped make the local populace feel more secure. As a Winchester resident noted, upon their arrival the town seemed to heave a sigh of relief, feeling that they were now "perfectly safe" from the enemy.[48]

Although the return of Jackson and his men eased the minds of many in regard to their personal safety, their presence did little to help the Valley inhabitants in their day-to-day existence. As they had already discovered, the war made what had once been the simplest of endeavors, such as putting food on the table, a harrowing experience. Within a very short time, the basic staples of everyday life, such as sugar, coffee, salt, and clothing were in short supply and priced beyond the reach of the average citizen. In mid-August coffee was selling for 25 cents a pound; in less than a month, the price more than doubled, and many families began using rye in their coffee as a way of stretching it. Salt also became a precious commodity; in late August it was selling for $8 a sack, and by the start of September it could not be had for any price. Three months later a sack cost $30. Even such commonplace items as matches demanded exorbitant prices. Before the war, a gross had retailed for less than 65 cents, but now an individual would have to spend at least $6 to acquire them; even then, they were in short supply. Fearful of not being able to obtain winter clothing when the time came, citizens began buying whatever could be found in August while it was still available. In Lexington, Mary White, unsuccessful in her attempts to locally secure a supply of salt, pepper, and coal oil for the upcoming winter, asked her father in Richmond to purchase whatever he could before he returned home.

As the lady of the house, Julia Chase realized that the current situation would only become more acute as time passed. "Our winter, I fear, will be rather a hard one," she wrote in her diary in August. "I hope we shall not have a severe one as regards the weather." In late September she wrote, "This war causes trouble in everything and way, in this part of Virginia. We are put to a great deal of inconvenience & expense to procure things." By December, after prices had risen still further, she declared in disgust, "If these are our rights we don't want such rights any longer, but restore us again to our former peace & Happiness."[49]

Other Valley residents were also distressed over the constant shortages and spiraling costs. With the availability of supplies uncertain, Reverend Brooke augmented his family's fare by stalking fowl in the surrounding countryside. "Spent the day in the country—hunting—brought home a nice lot of birds—they come in very well these scarce times." Araminta Trout, of Front Royal, complained to her daughter in Morgantown, Virginia, about the "great scarcity" of everything except bread. Alone out in the countryside, with her husband in the army, Rockbridge County resident M. C. Trevey in late November appealed to James Davidson for assistance in obtaining adequate sustenance. "I have ben getting some meet each week for a while, but the gentleman who furnished it has stopped butchering as I understand, so I have no meet at all. There is other nessarys of life that I need, but as bread & meet is the two main supporters of human life I would ask for them first."[50]

Concern about the future availability of supplies was surely the determining factor when farmers in the vicinity of Mount Jackson and Strasburg refused to sell their products to the government, except at extraordinarily high prices. Although minor in scope, this was a situation the authorities could not tolerate; to prevent it from becoming more widespread, the War Department acted quickly and decisively. In a dispatch on December 27, 1861, Secretary Benjamin notified General Johnston how he should respond to the situation:

> I am informed . . . that parties near Mount Jackson and Strasburg are refusing to sell their grain, & c., necessary for the subsistence of the Government cattle and hogs purchased for the supply of the Army, except at exorbitant prices. This state of things should not be tolerated. Our Army must be fed. The supplies necessary for this purpose must be had, and those who refuse to sell them to the Government at fair and reasonable rates cannot be regarded as true friends of the cause. You are, therefore, requested to issue orders requiring the impressment of such supplies, wherever the owners refuse to dispose of them at fair market value in Confederate money.[51]

The shortages and high prices provided fertile ground for smugglers to ply their trade. Outraged by the amount of illicit trading taking place, one Winchester resident, C. W. Price, issued a protest to the local military authorities, who in turn passed it along to the War Department in Richmond. Since the granting of passes into Maryland had long been forbidden, Price wondered why there continued to be a steady flow of individuals crossing the Potomac to conduct business north of the river. "There is a regular thoroughfare between this place and Hancock," he said, "and I think it should be stopped."

One individual engaged in such activity was Samuel Pancoast. A Quaker and New Jersey native who later moved south and resided in Hampshire County, Virginia, Pancoast spent much of his time in the Valley, and soon after the war began, he cleverly obtained permission to trade in salt from authorities on both sides of the Potomac. Throughout the summer, he never encountered any difficulty in crossing the river whenever and wherever he chose, which caused his fellow neighbors to wonder. He also never delivered a pound of salt south of the border, and by November the Confederate authorities had become wise to Pancoast's scheme and arrested him for collaborating with the enemy. He spent the next two years in prison in Richmond and Salisbury, North Carolina.[52]

As winter approached, those who had loved ones in the military—by now just about everyone in the Valley—became increasingly concerned about their welfare. Upset over the harsh conditions her son and the other troops had to endure, one Winchester mother, Mrs. Phillip Williams, sent a stinging letter to her son's commanding officer, Col. William Nelson Pendleton, asking him to help alleviate the hardships the soldiers were experiencing. Reuben Scott, stationed in Strasburg, tried to allay his wife's fears as to the suffering the army would experience during the upcoming winter by telling her that they were presently doing everything in their power to make living conditions as comfortable as possible. Some residents did everything they could to help their loved ones endure the winter, making and sending them warm clothing.[53]

Valley residents longed for the end of the conflict, still less than a year old, but they knew that the end of the war was not in sight. Julia Chase described the reality of the situation most accurately when she wrote in mid-December, "The War will I think commence now in earnest, what our future will be none can tell." Although she did not know it at the time, within the next six months, the Shenandoah Valley would become the battleground for one of the most spectacular and brilliant campaigns of the entire war, one that would forever immortalize Stonewall Jackson as a military hero. The Valley's inhabitants would also begin to experience firsthand the price they would have to pay in order to gain their independence.[54]

CHAPTER 4

"Friends Are No Better than Foes"

1862

Ｎew Year's Day, 1862, much to the delight of the Valley's inhabitants, dawned to unusually warm and windy skies. Keeping a daily meteorological record of the weather, Francis McFarland noted that the temperature almost reached sixty degrees. To Julia Chase in Winchester the day seemed "more like Spring than mid-winter." In Front Royal, Lucy Buck and her sisters could not resist the urge to go atop their house and watch "the lifting of the mist from the valley. How beautiful it looked, soft and white as a snow-wreath and braided with gold and crimson of the sunshine."[1]

The very next day the temperature dropped below freezing, where it would remain for a good part of the month; and in the following weeks the residents of the Valley had little else to look forward to but continued interludes of rain, sleet, snow, biting cold, and overcast skies. By the end of the month the dreariness of the elements seemed to be getting to Miss Chase. "Snow, rain, and with no prospect of fair weather," she dejectedly wrote in her diary, "we have scarcely had 6 pleasant days during the entire month of January."[2]

The bleak weather in the opening days of 1862 coincided perfectly with the mood of the Valley's populace. Lucy Buck expressed heartache when her cousins had to depart and return to camp during the first week of February. On their last day at home, she played backgammon with them, and later she knitted a cap for her cousin George, for which she received his warmest thanks. That evening they sat around the fireplace talking well into the night, but the sadness of the moment did not escape Lucy. Intent on saying good-bye, she awoke at three o'clock in the morning to see her cousins off. "They came in and stayed with us a few moments," she said, "and then with warm farewells and hearty good wishes they left us in the house very lonely."[3]

While the departure of loved ones was certainly reason enough for the Valley's inhabitants to be downcast, equally disheartening were the recent reverses experienced by the Confederate military forces in the field. The capture of Forts Henry and Donelson, plus the loss of Roanoke Island in North Carolina, followed soon after by the evacuation of Nashville, led many a citizen to wonder about the Confederacy's chances of prevailing in the struggle. Shortly after hearing of the capture of the two forts, Mary Scott wrote to her husband that she was tired of the war and looked forward to its end, though she did not see it coming to a satisfactory conclusion anytime soon, seeing as the tide presently was not in favor of the Confederacy. James D. Davidson wrote to a friend in mid-February that the only topic presently being discussed was the bad news from Roanoke Island and the disasters suffered in the west. Upon hearing of the Confederate setbacks, Mary White told her father, "The news from the west is very discouraging & we are all greatly depressed by it. News came to-day . . . that Yankees are in Nashville. We hope that this is not true." James White had an explanation for the South's recent lack of success: "We are rather dispirited by the bad news this morning," he said in the aftermath of the Roanoke debacle, "but it does no good to give play to anything like despondency . . . it seems to me that our people are not enough in earnest yet."[4]

Many of those in the ranks were not so easily discouraged, however. Frank Paxton, an officer in the Stonewall Brigade, wrote to his wife from camp on the outskirts of Winchester that she should not give much credence to reports of bad news. "All I can say is, do not be alarmed, and make up your mind to bear in patience whatever of good or evil the future may have in store for us. . . . The future is not so bright as it was before our late disasters, but we have yet many strong arms and brave hearts in the field, and should not despair." Richard Buck wrote to his mother in a similar vein: "I suppose the Roanoke disaster has very much disheartened the people. But we can not always be victorious. I think it will be of an advantage to the troops for we have been unaccustomed to defeats. . . . This will arouse them and teach them that we are fighting a largely superior force and a determined people."[5]

Although he was only seventeen, Richard Buck had correctly discerned that the troops were overconfident because of their earlier successes. It was a point that the newspapers picked up on as well. In fact, just before the Confederate reverses, the *Winchester Republican* reminded its readers that they would do well if they did not become too expectant of success. "To say that there is a possibility of our subjugation . . . we cannot believe. But if, sanguine of success, we slumber in our security, whilst the enemy surrounds us on all sides, they may secure a foothold from which it may require years of toil and thousands of lives and treasures to dispossess them." Following the Confederate misfortunes in Tennessee and North Carolina, the *Staunton Spectator* did its best to put a positive light on the current circumstances. "We are not disposed to take a gloomy view of the seemingly sad reverses with which our arms have recently met. We do not feel discouraged by them; on the contrary, we believe that they will eventually result in good to the cause of the South. . . . These reverses are but the thunder-claps which are necessary to arouse the giant of Southern energy from its false repose."[6]

One person who did not need to be aroused or encouraged was Stonewall Jackson. Jackson was aware of the Valley's importance and decided that he could best defend the region by launching an attack against the Federal troops stationed to the northwest. He also realized that considerable quantities of provisions could still be obtained in the counties immediately west of the mountains. He had relayed his thoughts to the secretary of war in late November 1861: "I deem it of very great importance that Northwestern Virginia be occupied by Confederate troops this winter. At present it is to be presumed that the enemy are not expecting an attack there, and the resources of that region necessary for subsistence of our troops are in greater abundance than in almost any other season of the year. Postpone the occupation of that section until spring, and we may expect to find the enemy prepared for us and the resources to which I have referred greatly exhausted." Consequently, soon after his arrival in Winchester, Jackson led his forces on an expedition to the northwest, to strike the Federal garrison at Romney and to obtain whatever supplies he could from the region.[7]

Jackson left Winchester on January 1, 1862, and returned three and a half weeks later. Despite a host of difficulties, among them the freezing weather, the campaign wound up being a success. Upon hearing of the Confederate advance, the Federals abandoned their position, leaving large amounts of stores and valuable medical supplies behind. The Confederates were just as successful in the second part of their mission. In the weeks following their occupation of the region, a constant stream of cattle and wagons loaded with supplies made their way across the mountains to Winchester. By the middle of February, Hawks reported to his superiors that all available subsistence had been secured from the territory.

Events in the west also affected what transpired in the Valley. Two days after the capture of Fort Donelson, Hawks received orders from Richmond to purchase all the bacon to be found in the Valley to offset the anticipated loss of supplies by the evacuation of middle Tennessee. So successful was Hawks in the procurement of foodstuffs that the Subsistence Department in the last week of February directed him to cease forwarding his purchases of flour to the army at Manassas, as they already had sufficient quantities on hand, and to send any more purchases, beyond what his command may need, to Charlottesville, where it would be stored.[8]

The Confederates were wise in spending much of their time and energy on collecting whatever resources they could during this time of repose. The harshness of winter was fast coming to an end, and active campaigning would begin shortly thereafter, a factor that certainly would hamper their efforts at gathering resources later on. Federal troops had been marauding on the northern fringes of the Valley for months, their boldness increasing with time, and there was no doubt as to what direction they would take when the time came. That time came soon. In late February, as part of the overall Federal offensive to capture Richmond, Maj. Gen. George B. McClellan, commander of the Army of the Potomac and the Department of the Potomac, which presently included the environs of Washington, D.C., Northern Virginia, and portions of Maryland, directed Maj. Gen. Nathaniel P. Banks to march south and drive the Confederates from Winchester and the Lower Valley. Banks and his army of approximately 28,000 crossed over the Potomac on February 24, took possession of Harpers Ferry, and by March 6 had advanced as far south as Bunker Hill, a scant 12 miles north of Winchester.

Jackson was vastly outnumbered—the total strength of his command did not exceed 5,400 men—and was compelled to vacate Winchester. Accordingly, on March 6 he ordered Hawks and army quartermaster John Harman to begin removing all supplies from the town. This directive did not come as a surprise to Hawks; anticipating such an eventuality, Jackson's chief commissary officer had ten days earlier directed his superiors in Richmond to send all future shipments for the army to Strasburg. He also took great pains to ensure that all reserve stockpiles at Strasburg were transferred to the safety of the depot at Mount Jackson. Because of the ability and perseverance of Harman and Hawks, when the Valley Army pulled out of Winchester, not a single piece of equipment or a pound of subsistence was left to the enemy, a fact that the commissary general made note of in a report to the secretary of war the following month.[9]

The Confederate retreat from Winchester began with the supply trains slowly weaving their way south along the Valley Pike during the afternoon of March 11. Later that evening, the infantry and artillery were signaled to form

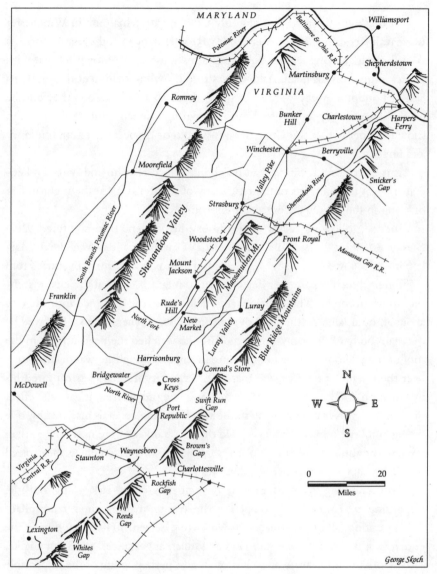

The Shenandoah Valley of Virginia.

ranks, and the troops exited the city. Dejected and reluctant to leave, Jackson waited until nearly midnight before joining the procession. Laura Lee, from her home on Cameron Street, watched sadly as the long columns of infantry marched out of town and disappeared into the darkness, knowing that come morning she and the rest of Winchester's residents would be on their own and at the mercy of the enemy.

At first light the next day, the only Confederate remaining in Winchester was cavalry commander Turner Ashby. Resplendent in full dress uniform, a colorful sash and fine leather belt around his waist, and a brown felt hat with a black plume on his head, Ashby sat astride his white stallion at the southern end of Loudoun Street waiting for the Federals to appear. When they did, he turned away slowly and trotted out of town in a defiant gesture designed to show the enemy that the Confederates were retiring because of circumstance and not fear.[10]

But the city's inhabitants had no choice but to remain, and with the Federal army at the outskirts of the city, many of them had spent the night in fear of being in the enemy's hands come morning.[11]

Indeed, following Ashby's colorful exodus, Federal troops entered Winchester. At about 8 A.M., an advance guard of cavalry made its way down Market Street, followed soon after by a squad of approximately forty infantry. From a different direction, another detachment of infantry entered the city, marching up Main Street. The Federal army made its grand entrance into the city about an hour later. At the head of the column was General Banks, followed by the main body of the army. Reverend Brooke watched the pageantry from the roof of the jailhouse, the tallest building in town. Though he was disheartened over the enemy's presence, the march into the city nevertheless captured his imagination: "When the sun struck the long line of bayonets, it gave the effect of a glittering silver river moving in the wind." As the Federals marched by, one young child, who must have been told that the Yankees were nothing less than the reincarnation of the devil himself, shouted out in amazement as they passed by, "Why, they look like people, don't they?"[12]

Not knowing what to expect, few citizens dared risk going outside. According to Laura Lee, except for the troops making their triumphant demonstration, all of the streets in town were deserted. "The town during the entrance of the troops presented a sad and sullen appearance," said John Clarke. "Many of the houses were entirely closed, few, perhaps none of the respectable portion of the town were conspicuous on the street."[13]

Once the Yankees had actually arrived, much of the townspeople's fear seemed to diminish, but their enmity and resentment most certainly did not. Having no choice but to accept the Northerners' presence, the citizens of Winchester, the ladies especially, were determined not to submit or give satisfaction to the enemy in any way, and there were frequent displays of anger and defiance.[14]

The contempt and hostility exhibited by a majority of the townspeople of Winchester following its occupation came as a surprise to the Federals. In a conversation with Cornelia McDonald, a soldier said that he was astonished to see the degree of bitterness leveled toward them by the people, the ladies in particular. "I do not think that since I have been here I have seen a pleasant countenance. I always notice that the ladies on the street invariably turn away their faces when I look at them, or if they show them at all, have on all their sour looks." McDonald told him that this was to be expected; it would be asking too much of the people to express feelings of joy while they were under the domination of their foe.[15]

The Yankees' bewilderment over not being welcome delighted Winchester's ladies. Doing everything she could to make the Federals feel as uncomfortable as possible, Laura Lee commented in her diary, "We are glad to hear that they are very much disappointed in their reception here. They say they were never treated with such scorn, as by the Winchester ladies." Unionist Julia Chase, though ecstatic that the Federals had taken possession of Winchester, could not believe how the majority of her fellow residents were treating them. "The Secesh. are bolder & bolder every day, and talk as saucy as they please. One of the gentlemen told me that the Ladies of Charlestown conduct themselves shamefully, actually stop, when they pass the Provost Guard & spit in their faces."[16]

But far more important to her at this moment was the condition and whereabouts of her father, who had been arrested by the Confederates just before their evacuation of the city. Appalled though they were by his arrest, it did not come as a shock to the family, who had been expecting it for days. Chase was not the only one to be incarcerated. A few days before they pulled out, the Confederates made a sweep of the town and surrounding countryside, arresting almost a score of Unionist supporters, among them one of Harriet Griffith's uncles, all of whom Jackson decided to take with him as prisoners when the army marched south.

For more than a month, families with members in custody of the Confederates heard little, other than rumors, as to what had become of them. First, reports said the men had been sent to Strasburg, then Harrisonburg, and finally, by mid-April, rumor had it that the men were behind bars in a Richmond prison. "We have sad news today, if true," said Julia, "that father has after all been carried to Richmond. . . . God grant the news may not be true; all hope is gone should F. be there." In an attempt to win their release, the Unionist citizens in

Winchester initiated two petitions, though they were not very hopeful that either would be successful. But then Jackson released the captives, and they arrived safely back in town on April 24, though haggard and much worn down. The men described the experiences they had to endure, which Julia compared to that of galley slaves.[17]

The Confederates were not the only ones guilty of such practices, however. The Federals also took a number of people into custody for exhibiting their support of the South. In her diary during February and March, Sarah McKown commented several times on how soldiers suddenly appeared and took people away. Arrests of individuals in Berryville and Shepherdstown became commonplace, and following the occupation of Winchester, a number of individuals suddenly found themselves behind bars. In most instances, those apprehended were detained for only a short period of time, usually just a few days. The majority understood as well that intimidation and fear were the motivating factors behind their arrests.[18]

Still, in spite of the arrests, Unionists were overjoyed by the Federals' presence. Having put up with taunts and insults from most of their neighbors for almost a year, Unionists viewed the Federal possession of the city as their liberation from the clutches of the enemy, and they were not about to restrain their feelings of happiness. When the Federal troops marched into the city, Unionist citizens welcomed them. Banners bearing the stars and stripes were displayed in front of a number of houses, and the ladies cheered and waved handkerchiefs as the soldiers passed by. Some, such as Harriet Griffith, welcomed the soldiers into their homes, feeding and entertaining them.[19]

The Confederate withdrawal from Winchester and the Unionists' outpouring of affection toward the Federal troops infuriated most loyal Southerners and heightened tensions between the two factions considerably. When it became known that one woman in town had "entirely taken the Northern side" and had become familiar with several Yankee officers, all of her friends refused to have anything more to do with her. When a minister finished preaching before his congregation, one of his parishioners refused to shake his hand, saying he was now his enemy, a feeling another member believed was the prevailing view among most of the church's members. The meanness now being exhibited by those on both sides saddened Reverend Brooke. He mused over the deplorable state of things: "I have not seen such enmity in my life—families separated—churches sundered—fanaticism rife—and the Devil in the heart of those we used to call Saints!" This hatred and anger would only increase in the days to come.[20]

As Julia Chase had predicted, the war had now begun in earnest. In their advance up the Valley at the onset of the campaign, Federal troops displayed complete disregard for the rights of the local inhabitants, and Southerners quickly discovered that the concept of personal property had lost all meaning. Soon after the Federals took possession of Berryville, Treadwell Smith had to put up with his residence being used as the headquarters for several officers and their staffs, among them Colonel McDowell of the 84th Pennsylvania Infantry. Immediately upon the Federals' arrival in Winchester, and in the weeks afterward, many citizens there also had to bear the indignity of having their homes occupied by Federal officers. Banks established the army's headquarters at the residence of George Seevers; General Shields used the domain of Mary MaGill for his quarters; and the commanding officers of Massachusetts regiment made themselves comfortable in the house of Mr. Mason, one of the town's leading citizens. Even Cornelia McDonald, who lived on the outskirts of town, did not escape the imposition of the enemy. Soon after the Federals took possession of the city, General Williams, one of Banks's division commanders, sent an aide to inquire about the possibility of setting up his headquarters at the McDonald homestead. Dismayed by the thought, Mrs. McDonald told the aide that she had seven children to care for, and at the moment the two youngest were ill. Not wanting to add to her burdens, the general said he would find accommodations elsewhere. But upon her return from town one day in April, she saw the Union flag flying over her front door. While she was in town on an errand, officers of the 5th Connecticut Infantry had occupied her house for their headquarters, and the entire regiment had taken up residence in her orchard. Incensed that the enemy had taken over her house, yet realizing there was little she could do, Mrs. McDonald nevertheless stated her objections to the commanding officer and asked him to remove the flag flying over the door. If he refused to do so, she declared, she would have to enter her own house from the rear. Wanting to make their stay as pleasant as possible, the officer had the flag moved to the side of the house.[21]

But as the people of Winchester were about to discover, the occupation of their homes by the enemy would turn out to be the least of their concerns. Since they were in hostile territory, the Federals did not feel obliged to respect the townspeople's property and consequently did not hesitate to appropriate anything they wanted when the mood struck. Many of the men bivouacked on McDonald's property augmented their fare by stealing chickens and milk from her cow almost daily. Mrs. McDonald noticed a short time later that one of the cedar trees flanking her driveway had been cut down for fuel for the soldiers' campfires.

Other soldiers also committed acts of thievery and vandalism. On the afternoon of the Federals' arrival, John Clarke ordered two soldiers out of his house after they entered uninvited, but not before they made off with several pieces of his silver service. That same evening, he discovered that at least sixty troopers of the 3rd New York Cavalry had moved into his barnyard. The soldiers took all of his hay and wood, leaving nothing for Clarke and his family. The next day, they broke into his storage sheds, knocked out a number of his fence boards for firewood, and quartered a dozen horses in his garden. When Clarke complained about the brazen attitude of the men toward the property of others, one of the soldiers stated rather indifferently, "Oh, that's a small matter. The country is broken up. It all belongs to Uncle Sam."

Many of the merchants in town also suffered terribly, as their products were constantly being pilfered by the troops that crowded the streets. Going into a store under the guise of purchasing a particular item, one or two soldiers would divert the shopkeeper's attention while several comrades pocketed whatever they could. To counteract this system of thievery, a number of merchants soon began exhibiting only one or two items at a time, making sure that those displayed were always within their line of sight. Outraged by the soldiers' behavior, one resident declared in disgust, "They steal everything they can lay their hands on."[22]

Shocked as they were by the depredations of the enemy, the citizens of Winchester actually had not fared too badly. They soon learned that the Federals had inflicted far worse devastation on their neighbors in the surrounding countryside. Every day, reports of farms being ransacked and destroyed circulated throughout the town. When the soldiers came upon the farm of Fayette Washington, they took or laid waste to everything he owned except for the clothes on his back. They broke his furniture, tore his carpets to bits, and threw away all of the family's personal letters. Another farmer, his fields and crops ravaged, called upon the soldiers to leave him enough seed so he could plant some corn come spring, but the men only laughed at his appeal and told him that they did not intend to allow the people to do any planting this year.

Aside from the wanton acts of destruction, the soldiers also made certain to confiscate all farm products and anything else that would benefit their enemy. They routinely carried off most, if not all, of a farmer's horses and livestock and whatever quantities of corn, wheat, oats, hay, and straw they found in his barn and storehouses. Disheartened after watching a large train of wagons filled with supplies come in from the countryside, John Clarke said: "It is heart-rending to see the innumerable wagons that have passed . . . today ladened with every variety of farm produce, fencing, timber, etc. They leave little behind when they take possession of a farm." This wholesale destruction of farms continued unabated for weeks, and it led Laura Lee to express her concern about how she and her neighbors would survive. "What is to become of us if things continue as they are for any length of time, we do not know. . . . Many people are worse off than we. The farmers are ruined, everything destroyed except the land."[23]

In command of the region, the Federals gave the same treatment to homes and farmsteads throughout the Lower Valley, and citizens complained bitterly over the actions of the enemy, saying that the soldiers were destroying or stealing anything and everything that came across their path.[24]

In their seemingly systematic plundering of the countryside, the Federals did not fail to deprive the local inhabitants of one other commodity they valued highly—their slaves. Aware of how important slaves were to a farmer in working his land or keeping his house in order, the soldiers made certain not to leave them behind. One woman told of the Yankees simply backing a wagon up to the door of the slaves' quarters at one farm, loading them up, and taking them away to Winchester. In many instances the slaves ran off on their own, realizing that the Federals' presence made it impossible for their owners to prevent their leaving. Unable to resist the temptation to be free, hundreds of slaves left their owners, many attaching themselves to the Federal army, and others fleeing to Winchester, where they loitered about the streets and took up residence among the numerous abandoned buildings and houses. By May the countryside in the Lower Valley was reported to be practically devoid of slave labor, with many families lacking a single servant.[25]

This mass exodus of slaves caught many an owner by surprise. The sudden departure of her slave Evan came as a shock to Laura Lee, who had believed that if any of her servants would have remained faithful, it would have been him. Conceding that the lure of freedom was difficult to resist, Laura still found it hard to comprehend why a slave would want to leave and thus expose himself to the "hardships and difficulties of a free negroes life."

Even more striking, however, was the demeanor of the slaves themselves. Now in a position to express their resentment about their condition, many did not hesitate to do so. Having just obtained his freedom, one slave in Frederick County retaliated against his former owner by leading a detachment of Federal soldiers to his farm, which they then proceeded to despoil. The slave of a Winchester resident had charges brought against him with the Provost Marshall's Office for striking her.[26]

As the spring of 1862 began, the Valley remained the scene of military operations, and the war's debilitating effects upon the vitality of the region only intensified in scope. Business enterprise continued its downward spiral, most household articles were in short supply, and those few items still found on store shelves brought a high price. Making a rare venture out to shop during the first week of April, Laura Lee found her selection limited. "I made a sickly little effort today at shopping," she said. "The first for months. Very little to buy, and less to buy with." The noticeable absence of commercial activity was apparent throughout the Valley. In many towns, stores and businesses, as well as schools, were closed.[27]

Farmers also were finding it increasingly more difficult to cultivate their land. With the Confederates retiring up the Valley and the Yankees ravaging many homes and farms, farmers throughout the region felt uneasy and threatened. Concerned for their crops and not wanting to contribute to the support of the enemy, some began to debate the wisdom of cultivating all their land and spoke of seeding only a limited number of acres. Encamped near Woodstock when April began, Confederate Frank Paxton wrote to his wife about the conditions now prevalent in much of the Valley: "The whole country bears the appearance of a funeral, everything is so quiet. In a ride yesterday along our lines, I scarcely saw any person moving about, and all work on the farms seemed to be suspended; many of the houses seemed to be deserted."

Farmers could do little to protect their crops from the ravages of the enemy, but to prevent the capture of their livestock, many of them elected to drive their horses, cattle, and other animals over the Blue Ridge Mountains to the protective confines of the Confederate interior. Aware of how essential sheep were in providing wool for the manufacture of clothing, the *Lexington Gazette* proclaimed that during these harrowing times, it was the duty of every citizen to send his flocks out of the reach of danger if there was even the slightest possibility that they might fall into the hands of the enemy. As April drew to a close a citizen from the Upper Valley who witnessed the drive firsthand reported that a "great deal of livestock of the Valley" had "been run across the mountains into E. Va. in the last two weeks or more.[28]

The farmers could not even find an ally in the weather. Snow and an inordinate amount of rainfall throughout the winter and early spring turned the countryside into a vast quagmire and prevented many from plowing and preparing their land in time for spring planting. The adverse conditions continued to plague farmers through April, at the end of which an Augusta County resident wrote: "There has been so much rain this spring . . . farmers have been scarcely able to plow their ground and as yet I know not of an acre of ground planted in corn in this whole county. Should the season be favorable from this time out I think there will be nothing like half the usual amt. of corn planted."[29]

Also hindering the efforts of those in the countryside were the actions of the governmental authorities in Richmond in calling out the militia and establishing a military draft. Virginia had been invaded on several fronts, and the Confederate forces needed to be reinforced. Secretary of War Judah P. Benjamin in early March called upon Governor Letcher to immediately summon and put into the field 40,000 of the state's militia. Realizing the urgency of the situation, Letcher did not hesitate in responding to Benjamin's request, and on March 12 he issued an executive order authorizing Confederate generals commanding in Virginia to call for militia and muster them into service.[30]

As had occurred the summer before, the Valley's militia did not answer the call to arms with any degree of alacrity. Although Jackson pronounced that they were turning out encouragingly, by March 21 only those from Shenandoah County and 500 from neighboring Augusta County had reported for duty at Mount Jackson. Watching other units report in the days following, Reuben Scott expressed disappointment when his county's militia failed to appear. "We are looking for the Rockingham Militia . . . ," he told his wife, "but they are like a dog's *tail* always behind and I am sorry for it." In the end, it mattered little how long it took for the militia to report. Anyone who held back or refused to report would soon be liable to the military draft currently being considered in the Confederate Congress.[31]

After almost a year of conflict, the dreams of fame and glory envisioned by those who had volunteered at the war's start had since given way to its dreary realities, and most anxiously awaited the day when their enlistment expired and they could go home. In Company D, 33rd Virginia Infantry Regiment, of the famed Stonewall Brigade, forty-five of sixty-eight volunteers refused to reenlist when asked. "Ma, the romance of the thing is entirely worn off, not only with myself but with the whole army," wrote one veteran of the brigade. Another Valley soldier told his father that the generals were urging the men to volunteer again in the strongest terms, but he was leery and wanted to return home when his time expired. Pvt. George Harlow told his wife, "If I live this twelve months out, I intend to try mighty hard to keep out of [the army]. . . . I don't think I could stand it another year."[32]

Aware of the soldiers' discontent, the Confederate Congress in December had passed legislation it believed would persuade one-year volunteers already in the ranks to reenlist. Entitled the Furlough and Bounty Act, the law granted a $50 bounty and a sixty-day furlough to any soldier and noncommissioned officer who reenlisted for three years or the duration of the war. As further inducement, the bill permitted the men to join the branch of the service they wanted, transfer to a different company if they did not like the one assigned to, and elect new officers if they so desired.[33]

Designed to alleviate the army's shortage of manpower, this well-intentioned but misguided law actually created more problems, while solving none. Upon examining all its details, Confederate historiographer Douglas Southall Freeman concluded, "A worse law could hardly have been imposed on the South by the enemy." Instead of adding men to the ranks, the law, when implemented, did the exact opposite. Given the opportunity of putting $50 in their pockets and getting sixty-day passes, thousands of men signed their reenlistment papers and immediately took off on furlough. By March the Valley Army, which on paper claimed a strength in excess of 13,500 men, in fact mustered only 5,400 men of all arms.

Worse still, the measure threatened to undermine the command structure of the army. Officers who discharged their duties seriously and enforced rigid discipline were certain under the new regulations to be replaced by others who would be less inclined to do so. Stationed along the South Carolina coast at the time of its passage, General Lee deemed the law as written to be extremely detrimental to the Southern cause, and he shuddered at the consequences that might befall the army come spring. The reorganization of troops during times of peace, he said, was wasteful and time-consuming even under the best of circumstances; to attempt it during wartime in the face of an advancing enemy was unheard of and would in all likelihood result in disaster. Lee felt that the Confederacy would best be served by placing its troops under one unified command "organized for the war . . . be it long or short." Realizing the need for competent officers, he urged that they be appointed by the president and Congress and not be subject to a popularity contest among the men.[34]

President Davis agreed with Lee's recommendations, and on March 28, 1862, he sent Congress an official message advocating conscription. Though a number of Congress's members argued that the measure ran contrary to the basic tenet the Confederacy was fighting for, present military circumstances really left them no other recourse, and on April 16 the Confederate Congress passed the first conscription act in American history.[35] The act stated that all white men between the ages of eighteen and thirty-five were subject to military service for three years; those already in the army would be required to serve two more. This compulsory service was not as all-encompassing as it seemed, however. A drafted individual could evade his responsibility by hiring a substitute to take his place from those not liable for duty. Also, those who worked in occupations deemed vital to the war effort were excused from military service. Relenting to pressure, Congress exempted a wide range of vocations: all Confederate and state civil officials, teachers, druggists, hospital personnel, and those in a number of industrial professions including iron and railroad workers, blacksmiths, tanners, miners, and shoemakers.[36]

Stirred in large part by the urgings of Lee and Governor Letcher, Virginia's General Assembly had enacted similar legislation two months earlier that was identical to the national act in many ways, offering a $50 bounty to all volunteers, allowing them to join the company of their choice, and extending them a thirty-day grace period. The bill proclaimed all able-bodied white men eighteen and over liable to service in the militia, but the state's law extended the age limit of those eligible to forty-five. All those not in the army and who had not come forward by March 10 would have their names entered into a pool from which they could be conscripted to fill state volunteer units. The *Staunton Spectator* exhorted all those affected to avoid the stigma of being drafted—to do their patriotic duty and come forward.[37]

Having no real choice, most of the Valley's young men entered the service, either by volunteering or being drafted. There were exceptions, however, including workers in professions exempted under the law and a small number of individuals fortunate enough to hire substitutes. Also resistant to serving in the army were members of some religious denominations. When faced with conscription, those who could afford to do so hired replacements, a number attempted to try to make their way north to friends or relatives, and others reported to duty determined that they would not shoot when ordered. Jackson was fully aware of their unwillingness to serve, and while saying that they could be made to fire, he acknowledged that they could very easily take bad aim. Jackson sent out details to rack down and arrest all offenders who deserted or attempted to go north. He recommended that the War Department employ all those who refused to take up arms as teamsters, thus allowing the army to retain their services while at the same time respecting their religious beliefs and perhaps endearing them to the Confederate cause.[38]

Conscription was successful in augmenting the army's ranks. Nationwide, over 200,000 men were added to the rolls; in Virginia, the figure ran into the tens of thousands. But the policy deprived the agricultural community of most of its labor force, and nowhere was this more evident than in the Valley. After making the rounds in Warren County, one local resident maintained that the conscript officer had raked the county clean with a fine-tooth comb in his search for recruits, leaving behind only feeble old men and small boys unfit for military service. Many Valley families despaired of having their farms cultivated this year.

Traveling about Augusta County, Francis McFarland commented in his diary on how greatly troubled the people were about the militia being called out; as for his own situation he was distressed to learn that his son James had reenlisted for the war's duration. With her one son still at home now subject to military service, the sister of former Congressman John T. Harris expressed her concern over how the family would survive. If he was drafted, she told her brother, "I don't see what is to become of us." William Hooke informed his son Franklin that the family was "very badly off here at home"; little work had been done on the farm since he had left, and it would "be a hard matter to get out a spring crop."[39]

Though resentment to the draft was widespread, the Confederate government had no other alternative, given the circumstances. Fighting an unlimited war with limited means, they had to make hard choices, and the needs of the military understandably took precedence over the needs of individuals. The armies in the field ultimately had to be maintained if they were to win the war. By instituting a draft, however, the government was, as many of its leaders knew, only solving one problem at the expense of another—one they knew full well would come back to haunt them in the future.

⊱───◇───◆───⊰

Now more than 130 years distant in our national heritage, the Confederate Shenandoah Valley campaign of 1862 continues to command the attention of scholars, historians, and military strategists. In overall strategy and tactics, as well as generalship, the campaign ranks as one of the foremost and most spectacular of the entire conflict. Between May 8 and June 9, Jackson's forces traversed the Valley in its entirety, not once but twice, and in a series of brilliant maneuvers defeated three different Federal armies in five distinct engagements. Marching more than 350 miles during the campaign, at times being driven by their commander almost to the point of collapse, the Valley Army soon came to be known as Jackson's foot cavalry. The campaign was a classic example of using speed, deception, and knowledge of the terrain to counteract an enemy's superiority of numbers, and it has received high praise from scholars ever since and continues to be studied in military academies to this day.

The effects of the campaign were immediate. Jackson's exploits, coming on the heels of a string of Confederate defeats, electrified the Southern populace and raised their morale when most desperately needed. Even more important, they completely dismantled the Federal military plan of operation in Virginia. Because of the perceived threat to Washington City and in an attempt to defeat Jackson, troops scheduled to be sent to McClellan on the Peninsula were diverted to the Valley. In the end, Jackson eluded his potential captors, united with Lee outside of Richmond, and helped drive the Union forces back from the Confederate capital, while the troops slated to reinforce McClellan floundered in northern Virginia.[40]

Although Valley residents were ecstatic over the Confederate victories, the campaign proved to be unsettling in a number of ways. With two armies marching about the region, and the sound of gunfire and artillery constantly heard in the distance, anxiety over their well-being increased considerably. The women, who were at home alone with the children, totally defenseless, and without any idea of what was going on around them, felt cut off and abandoned, and they feared for their safety.[41]

Dampening the spirits of the people further were the actions of the Federals as they continued to go about the countryside laying waste to farms and homesteads during the course of the campaign and in the weeks to follow. Farmers throughout the Valley could do nothing but watch in dismay as the Yankees confiscated their horses and livestock and helped themselves to their provisions. "Poor Father," Lucy Buck said upon watching him labor in the fields under the hot sun. "I'm afraid he's harvesting his wheat only for the Yankees to take it from him afterwards."[42]

Even more disheartening were the large numbers of casualties coming in from the battlefield. Jubilant over being released from the clutches of the enemy, the residents of Winchester turned out en masse to welcome their liberators. But the joy of being free from their oppressors quickly turned to that of sadness when the wagons began to roll in with the dead and wounded. Mrs. Francis Barton was greeted by her son David, who had the gruesome task of telling his mother that his older brother, Marshall, had been killed in battle, shot in the neck. Another of Winchester's youth to be cut down on the field of battle was Powell Conrad, nephew to convention delegate Robert Conrad. Traveling to Winchester a few days later to pay her respects to the family, Matthella Page Harrison had a hard time accepting the young man's death and, with deep heart felt emotion, she declared, "Poor Powell, I cannot realize he has passed away." Throughout the Valley, family members were grief stricken to learn of the death of sons, husbands, and fathers.[43]

And yet in many cases, the sight or reports of those killed or wounded failed to elicit a tearful or emotionally charged response, as people had simply by its overwhelming presence become hardened to the war and its realities. In late May, Mrs. Margaret Preston of Lexington wrote matter of factly in her diary: "Heard today of a son of Dr. Breckenridge being killed at Shiloh; also, a cousin of Mr. P. being desperately wounded. Two dead soldiers passed through Lexington today. Last week *eight* dead bodies passed through. We are getting so used to these things, that they cease to excite any attention." Present when a soldier under Jackson first learned that his cousin had been killed in the fighting outside of Winchester, Mrs. Hugh Lee wrote of how distressed the young man had appeared, but then commented, "Such is war; such is life & death, as connected with it."[44]

The Valley's inhabitants had also become accustomed to the presence of military agents engaged in the process of accumulating supplies for the army. Indeed, to enhance their ability in collecting all possible subsistence from the region, commissary officials in Richmond, showing keen wisdom and insight, had the previous spring taken the judicious step of hiring citizens from the Valley and the surrounding counties to act as agents for the department.[45]

The press and a number of leading citizens, proud of what the Valley had contributed to the cause during the first twelve months of the war, and motivated in part by a desire to obtain additional military protection, thought it would again be prudent to remind the government of the Valley's importance and agricultural prowess. Toward that end, the *Lexington Gazette* in May 1862 called attention to the fact that the Valley for the past decade had been the most productive section of the state and could practically by itself support the Confederate armies operating in Virginia. Using the 1850 census statistics—the latest available—as evidence, the paper pointed out that the region produced over 25 percent of the state's total harvest in wheat and hay, as well as substantial quantities of corn, oats, rye, barley, and potatoes, and raised in aggregate value at least 20 percent of the state's livestock. The region was also the leading manufacturer of three other resources the Confederacy desperately needed: iron, lead, and salt.[46]

Two others who concurred with the *Gazette's* analysis were Alexander H. H. Stuart and Andrew Hunter. Pondering the future, and wondering how the armies were to be fed, Stuart advocated that the government take advantage of the vast resources currently in the Upper Valley, warning that if the Confederates failed to do so, the Federals would certainly put them to good use. "The counties of Augusta, Rockingham, and Rockbridge now abound with supplies of wheat, flour, corn, pork, bacon, cattle, and sheep. Last year's crop of corn and wheat were the largest ever raised in those counties, and the growing crops are remarkably promising. . . . Should the enemy get possession of the Upper Valley they will gain supplies sufficient to maintain a large army for twelve months to come. If, on the other hand, we can drive them out, these supplies can be applied to the sustenance of our own troops."

A short time later, Andrew Hunter voiced similar concerns to the secretary of war: "Beyond question there is now being harvested in that quarter (if it can be saved) the finest wheat crop that ever grew even in that productive Valley; and . . . notwithstanding the ravages of the enemy and the heavy drafts made upon it by our own armies, there is still a large quantity of meats, both beef and bacon, yet to be found there." Putting the matter in perspective, Hunter, in closing, posed a most appropriate question: "Now sir, should the war be prolonged beyond the coming autumn, could we afford to lose these resources? . . . can we get along without them?"[47]

Stuart's and Hunter's concerns were largely without merit, however. Though unable to provide Jackson with any additional forces, the authorities in Richmond had no intention of relinquishing the Valley or any of its considerable resources to the enemy—at least not willingly. President Davis said as much to General Johnston in a dispatch on February 28, in which he stated his regret at not having the requisite manpower to assist Jackson, as well as his desire for the Confederacy to maintain control of the region. "The letter of General Jackson presents the danger with which he is threatened and the force he requires to meet it. It is unnecessary for me to say that I have not the force to send, and have no other hope of his re-enforcement than by the militia of the valley." As for retaining the possession of the area, he told Johnston, "Anxious as heretofore to hold and defend the valley, that object must be pursued as to avoid the sacrifice of the army now holding it or the loss of the arms in store and in use there." Still, the uncertainty of events did not discourage the Confederates from taking advantage of the Valley's resources. Come spring, agents of the Commissary and Quartermaster Departments, as well as Hawks and others, continued to go about the countryside purchasing whatever provisions they could find. By May Hawks and his fellow officers had acquired substantial amounts of flour and bacon and had rounded up 10,000 head of cattle, to be used for the troops defending the Confederate capital.[48]

During the Valley Campaign, Jackson's army for the most part lived off the immediate countryside, securing whatever supplies they needed as they traveled. Hawks's records seem to confirm this point. For May and most of June, his papers are fragmentary, showing only intermittent purchases of provisions. But in a partial statement for the last week of June, when the fighting had ceased and Hawks and his staff could resume their duties, his papers show purchases of more than 500 head of cattle, 2,100 barrels of flour, and 60,000 pounds of bacon.[49]

In the ensuing months, officials of the Commissary Department directed Hawks to increase his efforts. On July 3, in response to a dispatch received a few days earlier, Commissary General Lucius B. Northrop instructed Hawks to acquire all the flour, beef, and bacon he could from the region. A month later, an aide to Northrop sent Hawks a communiqué telling him to gather up a supply of bacon from the surrounding countryside for use in sustaining the valley army and not to look to either Richmond or Lynchburg as a source of subsistence. Hawks received yet another directive from Northrop five days later, instructing him to purchase all the wheat he could and to "have it carried to safe places where it will be entirely safe from attacks of the enemy and at the same time will be available to us."[50]

Hawks established a supply depot just outside of Gordonsville, beyond the effective reach of the enemy and along the Virginia Central Railroad in order to facilitate the transportation of goods, and he and his limited staff went about the Valley pursuant of their orders. To provide Hawks with the necessary capital to carry out his responsibilities, the Commissary Department in Richmond between July and November allocated and forwarded more than $1 million. Hawks put this money to good use. During this five-month period alone, he secured for the army more than 8,200 barrels of flour, 15,000 head of cattle, and 240,000 pounds of bacon, traversing the entire length of the Valley, and obtaining provisions in at least nine different locations between Staunton and Harpers Ferry. Most of these supplies were then promptly transferred to the storage depots at Gordonsville, Charlottesville, and Lynchburg for distribution and safekeeping.[51]

Hawks generally encountered little resistance when requisitioning supplies. Valley farmers generally were parting willingly with any surplus quantities of meat and grain. Typical was Francis McFarland, a farmer who in August sold a considerable portion of his excess flour to the government. McFarland was even so accommodating as to transfer his ten barrels of flour into government sacks and deliver them at his own expense to the commissary post at Staunton.

The farmers were not always cooperative, however. By the fall of 1862, bacon was fast becoming a precious and coveted commodity, and with an eye on the coming winter, a growing number of farmers, while willing to support the military, were reluctant to part with surplus bacon. Hawks overcame their reluctance by offering to exchange government salt for bacon, a trade he knew most would find hard to pass up, as they would not be able to preserve their supply of meat for winter without it.

Troubles also arose in regard to the price of flour. Hawks and the other Confederate agents operating in the Valley were currently offering $7.50 to $8 per barrel, a figure many farmers believed to be unfair and far below the present market value, as flour was selling in the Confederate capital for roughly two and a half times that price.[52]

Following the Battle of Antietam and the subsequent Confederate withdrawal from Maryland, the Valley once again became the focal point of military operations, as Lee and the Army of Northern Virginia encamped in the countryside around Winchester. There, for the next five weeks, the troops recuperated from the summer campaigns. In late October Lee divided his army, taking the 1st Corps east of the Blue Ridge and leaving the 2nd Corps, under Jackson, in the Valley.[53]

Sprawled out across the Lower Valley, the Confederate presence prevented the Federals from inflicting any further damage on local homesteads, for which farmers were grateful, but after eighteen months of warfare, they also knew that in most instances it mattered little which color of uniform they were under; the end results were the same. Upon their arrival, the Confederates, like the Yankees before them, took over the fields, pastures, meadows, orchards, and woods of farms throughout the region. Though not intentionally seeking to cause their fellow citizens any harm, the troops did just that, as they scoured the local countryside in search of provisions, taking anything and everything they could use. For most of October, Gen. D. H. Hill's division of infantry was quartered on the property of William Abbott, of Frederick County. While encamped on Abbott's property, the soldiers trampled his wheat fields and appropriated over 3,100 fence rails and stakes, 1,600 fence posts, 50 cords of seasoned wood, 100 bushels of corn, four hogs, as well as his brood sire, and most of the hay from his barn. In Clarke County, a portion of Tredwell Smith's land was taken over by several units of cavalry for more than a month. During the first two weeks of November, Gen. A. P. Hill's division of tired and hungry soldiers invaded the farm of Charles Smith, of Berryville.[54]

By the fall of 1862, the Valley was no longer a landscape of peaceful, well-kept villages and towns, and farms with lush fields of wheat and corn, barns and storehouses full of grain, and pastures teeming with livestock. War's devastation was readily apparent. In a letter to a loved one back home in Mississippi, James Steptoe, a veteran of the army, described how Winchester and the countryside around it appeared at the end of September:

I am now in a country where my first aspirations towards military glory were indulged in. In this once gorgeous but, now desolate, valley, I began my soldiers career. . . . It is really heart rending to look at this county. There is scarcely a corn field for miles to relieve the waste and dreary monotony. Added to this, there had been no rain here for so long, that all the spontaneous growth of the country has been dried up. Most of the once familiar faces are gone and their firesides despoiled. Love, who has never known of the horrors of this war . . . enjoy a perfect elysium to these unfortunate people whose country has been successively ravaged first by one army and then another, for friends are no better than foes, when they come in the numbers that we move with. . . . And poor old Winchester, how I pity it! Once so gay, so pretty, and above all so true. Its glory has fled, I fear forever, for long years cannot restore it to its former loveliness. . . . Much of it has been burnt. Of what remains, is so filthy that one who has known it in better days, turns from it with pity and disgust.[55]

Jedediah Hotchkiss, the army's topographical engineer, wrote from his encampment at Bunker Hill, 12 miles north of Winchester, to his brother back home in Augusta County, "[The] country is almost destitute of every kind of forage or subsistence, for it has been full of armies for a long time." Valley resident Margaret Russell observed in November: "The soldiers are all over this neighborhood. The citizens are nearly devoured. If they feed and forage here all winter as they are now doing sad will be their condition when Spring comes tis bad enough now." In fact, by mid-October, division commissary officers already had to travel as far south as Front Royal, more than 20 miles from Winchester, to obtain flour.[56]

The continued presence of military forces picking the countryside clean led to a considerable increase in war weariness among the Valley's inhabitants. In the forefront of the fighting for more than a year, they had come to despise the war and all the pain and misery that accompanied it. What appalled them the most were the staggering numbers of killed or wounded, which they knew would only increase as the fighting continued. The engagements of second Bull Run and Antietam were extremely hard fought and bloody. In their aftermath, families and friends up and down the Valley received the heartbreaking news that loved ones had been killed, and the Valley once again became inundated with thousands of wounded. "This has been the most awful day we have ever spent," said Winchester resident Laura Lee three days after the battle of Antietam. "Directly after breakfast the lines of ambulances began to come in, and since then it had been an incessant stream. 3,000 wounded men have been brought in. Every place is crowded with them, and it is perfectly heart rending to know how much suffering and misery there is around us." In Lexington and the immediate countryside alone more than a half dozen households lost family members. The Preston family, who after the wounding of their older child three months earlier, now had to grieve the loss of their younger son, Willy, who was mortally wounded on the field at Manassas. The news of this death devastated the entire family, and the long list of those killed, many of whom she had known since they were little children, so devastated Mrs. Preston that she cared little as to the outcome of the war. "It is like the death of the first born in Egypt. Who thinks of or cares for victory now!"[57]

With major portions of the Lower Valley having changed hands a number of times since the start of hostilities, tensions between Unionist and Confederate citizens intensified considerably. When the Confederates were in control, citizens still loyal to the Union were harassed, their homes were routinely searched for contraband, and the more outspoken were often detained or arrested on the most frivolous of charges. When the Federals were in control, the roles were reversed. They ransacked private residences and businesses, and arrested citizens for the slightest offense. What made all this even more distasteful was that the authorities were often directed to their subjects by fellow citizens.[58]

What infuriated the Confederate populace even more was a military order issued by Federal commander John Pope in the latter part of July obligating all male citizens currently residing within Federal lines to take an oath of allegiance to the United States. All who declined would be escorted south of the picket line and if found again within the confines of Northern jurisdiction, they would be considered spies and be subject to military law. Though never strictly enforced, the directive caused a considerable amount of consternation, as many knew they would be unable to care for their families if forced to leave. But despite the possible consequences, most Valley citizens refused to take the oath. Though a few were exiled or sent north as prisoners, most were generally treated like John Clarke, who declined to take the oath and was placed under house arrest for a short time.[59]

Demoralizing for all concerned were the shortages of provisions. Traveling to Charlestown in September for supplies, Matthella Page Harrison returned home disappointed, as there were few goods to be found in town. Inured as they were by now to hardship, the residents of Winchester nevertheless found it hard to accept the prices they had to pay for even the most basic of necessities. Bacon, when it could be found, sold for 50 cents a pound; a like quantity of sugar commanded a price of $2.50; a bushel of potatoes went for $8.00; a bushel of corn meal sold for $2.00; and a cord of wood exacted a price of $12.00 or more. Resigned to paying ever higher prices, a lady in Winchester best summed up the reality of the situation she and her fellow residents found themselves in when she said, "We are paying Richmond prices for articles now." Indeed, by this time, few Valley residents had any idea how they were going to make it through to spring. Margaret Preston echoed the concerns of many when she wrote: "What is to become of the country? The fear is that there is not enough food in it to keep the people from starving." Another Lexington citizen, James D. Davidson, wrote to his son, "There is a prospect of a little famine. There seems to be much uneasiness." The ability of Valley inhabitants to survive the winter was made even more precarious by the presence of the Confederate army. "Should this Army remain here all winter," Julia Chase wrote, "we shall certainly suffer very much, indeed there will be some danger of a famine."[60]

With adequate subsistence becoming harder and harder to come by, appeals for less fortunate citizens became more common. Newspapers throughout the Valley also called for Valley citizens to donate whatever they could— shoes, blankets, and clothing in particular—to the army so the troops, now in desperate need, would not freeze during the upcoming winter.[61]

Even more distressing than the fact that so many were facing such hard times was a seeming lack of concern by many over their plight. W. Frazier, a resident of Rockbridge County, wrote to James D. Davidson: "The destitution in our Army especially in the matter of shoes & clothing calls loudly for the most vigorous effort and liberal contribution on the part of the *people*. If the Government is slack in their performance of *its* duty to the soldiers, let not the same charge lie at *our* door." He continued, "There are few noble men in Rockbridge who, I doubt not have done & are doing their whole duty to the army in the field & in the hospitals, & to the poor at home. But these few are *the exceptional cases*." Another Rockbridge resident wrote in the *Lexington Gazette* about the "business of merchandizing" on the part of both farmers and merchants, who charged whatever they could get for their products, indifferent to their neighbors' suffering or condition. Greed had indeed become a corrupting influence, to the point that it was responsible for the creation of a new entrepreneurial class: the speculators. In existence since the war began, these individuals would go about the countryside and buy up at a fraction of their value all the corn, wheat, flour, pork, bacon, and other goods, store it away, and sell it later for an exorbitant price. Despised by all, the speculators had come to be looked upon by citizens as the cause of much of their suffering. But what was even more frustrating to many Valley residents was the fact that a considerable number of their neighbors were willingly selling their products to the speculators.[62]

Several other, far more substantial, factors were responsible for the current economic situation, however. The constant presence of the military had devastated Valley farms. And with the Federals in control of the Lower Valley a majority of the time, the Confederates were largely denied any surplus supplies from Berkeley, Clarke, Frederick, and Jefferson Counties. This was a major blow to the Confederates, as in 1860 these four counties alone accounted for 50 percent of the Valley's total wheat harvest.[63]

Another major factor was the weather. In the summer of 1862, the Upper South was subject to a severe drought, which led to a precipitous decline in crop production. While near Harrisonburg toward the end of October, Jedediah Hotchkiss made note of the drought's effect in his diary: "It is very dry, and hardly any seeding has been done, the Great Valley is almost destitute from the drought." He again commented on the dry conditions five days later when passing by the battlefield of Cross Keys: "The people are seeding with much difficulty, the ground is so dry."[64]

Commissary General Lucius B. Northrop sent a dispatch to the secretary of war in November, describing the situation as critical and informing the secretary that the wheat crop in Virginia was only one-fourth of what it had been the year before. He predicted nothing short of ruin for the Army of Northern Virginia if further provisions were not forthcoming. Worse still, because of enemy encroachments, there was nothing he could do to rectify the problem. "The chances of procuring sufficient supplies are becoming every hour more and more doubtful, and the area of country drawn from smaller and smaller. I am powerless to remedy the evil." The outlook for corn was even more grim. In the Valley, the heavy winter snows and spring rains, coupled with the drought during the summer and fall, caused the harvest to be extremely small.[65]

As for the shortages of beef, bacon, and pork, a number of factors also were to blame. The military forces and the agents of the Commissary Department had taken all excess livestock from the Valley since the start of the war. On November 3, 1862, Northrop's chief aide, Maj. Francis G. Ruffin, informed him that the Army of Northern Virginia had nearly exhausted the supplies of fresh beef, and he did not believe there would be enough to last till the end of the year. "Whether there will be adequate supplies for the Army of North-western Virginia depends very much on the size of that army. The fear of inva-sion and the waste of the army, never to be sufficiently blamed, have driven out many stock from that section, as evidenced by the fact that I have seen some seen cattle from there in this market from eighteen months to two years old, a thing never heard of before." Two weeks later, in his yearly report on subsis-tence to the War Department, Northrop wrote: "The number of beeves from all sources now available for General Lee's army, which now consumes 1,000 head per week, does not this day exceed, so far as this Bureau knows, 8,500 head; and over 4,000 of them are about 250 miles removed from him at this time, and winter is at hand." In addition, the summer drought had left the cat-tle so thin that the same number of animals did not go as far in supplying the troops as they had the year before. Even more discouraging, Northrop had lit-tle idea where subsequent supplies would come from. "The future of beef sup-ply for the Army," he said, "is so nearly exhausted that this Bureau does not know whence more is to be obtained."[66]

The situation was just as troubling, if not more so, when it came to pork and bacon. Because of the war's hardships, Valley farmers had been unable to raise nearly as many hogs as they had the year before. The *Rockingham Register* reported that the total number raised in the county was less than half that of the previous season. The drought and excessive heat had had a negative impact as well. With less corn and hay available to be used as feed, hogs could not be fat-tened, which meant smaller yields of bacon and pork. To make matters even worse, hog cholera had become widespread throughout the state and eventu-ally proved fatal to the state's entire population. According to the Subsistence Department, the entire supply of hogs in both North Carolina and Virginia did not exceed 20,000, and they too were smaller than in previous years because of the drought. Compounding the problem further, the department did not have enough salt to pack all the pork that it could obtain.[67]

The decline of the Valley as a viable source of supply for the Confederacy is reflected in a dispatch Lee sent on October 1 to Gen. Gustavus W. Smith, commander of the forces at Richmond. In attempting to predict the future movement of the Federal army, he told his fellow officer: "Whatever move-ment they do make into Virginia this fall, I think they will make vigorous effort to destroy the Central railroad, especially if they determine to advance up this Valley, as they consider that this army is dependent on that road for its supplies." He penned a similar letter to the secretary of war later the same day, saying, "Should they determine to advance into Virginia by the Shenandoah Valley, their great object will be to destroy the Virginia Central railroad, upon which they think we depend for our supplies."[68]

By the end of 1862, the Confederate authorities in Richmond were facing a severe crisis: Virginia could no longer provide enough subsistence to support the military forces in the field. The state's resources of both grains and livestock had been depleted, the Valley included. To the Subsistence Department, the Valley was just one of several regions of the state in which the farmers' productive capabilities had been so decimated by the war that they could no longer be depended upon to provide the Army of Northern Virginia with the large quantities of provisions it needed. In late November 1862, Northrop told the secretary of war, "Every source within Confederate lines from which supplies could have been obtained . . . have been fully explored. All such have either been exhausted or found inadequate. . . . Besides, large local supplies have been completely exhausted, as in Londoun, Fauquier, and other districts." Another report, issued by Northrop in January 1863, also confirmed the degree to which supplies in Virginia had been depleted: "Fifteen months ago, this Bureau foresaw that the supply of cattle in Virginia would be exhausted, and initiated an arrangement to bring hither cattle from Texas. . . . The attempt was made and failed. . . . Supplies cannot be gathered in the country southwest of General Lee's army. It has been or is being drained already. Nor can they be had on the south side of the James River. That country is held tributary in commissary supplies to Petersburg and the south (except in hogs), and even if they were (as they are not), in quantity to feed General Lee's army, they could not be had; neither time nor transportation will allow it."[69]

As the year came to an end, the Valley inhabitants were in low spirits. Margaret Preston lamented, "The sadness of the household forbids any recognition of Christmas; we are scattered to our own separate rooms . . . and the Library is in darkness." Laura Lee expressed similar sentiments in her diary on New Year's Eve: "A sad and dismal time, weather dark and gloomy, and every one more depressed than I have ever seen them. . . . There seems to be no hope of relief from our dismay."[70]

Sadness and despair had become the prevailing moods in many a Valley household. These feelings would only become more pronounced in the days and months ahead.

CHAPTER 5

"Alas! When Is the End to Be?"

1863

Immediately upon their return in December, the Federals had resumed their practices of harassing individuals and plundering homesteads. Two weeks into the new year, Yankee cavalry had already staged raids as far south as Woodstock, 30 miles south of Winchester, and by the end of February, they had swept through Berryville and the adjacent countryside half a dozen times.[1]

The return of the Union army also precipitated another mass departure of slaves from the region. Officially released from bondage when the Emancipation Proclamation took effect at the start of the year, large numbers of slaves anxious to experience their newfound freedom quickly packed up what few belongings they had and left. This exodus went on for weeks. To ensure that slaves were aware that they were free and could leave at any time, the Federals in their travels about the countryside made it a point to tell them. And in Winchester, copies of the proclamation were posted on practically every street corner, which inflamed many of the town's residents.[2]

Winchester residents had more pressing concerns, however. The new Federal commander, Brig. Gen. Robert H. Milroy, assumed command on January 1, 1863. Although he was in command for less than six months, Milroy would become the most despised and infamous of all the Union officers who presided over the city during the war. It was clear that his reign would be harsh from the day he arrived, when he let it be known that he expected the people to comply with the military order requiring them to take an oath of allegiance to the United States; individuals who refused would have troops quartered in their homes, and only those who had taken the oath would be permitted to purchase supplies from the shops and sutlers about town or travel to Maryland for provisions. Even they were restricted, allowed only to purchase enough for their own use. Two days later, he issued a directive putting a curfew into effect; no citizen was allowed out on the streets after 8:00 P.M. except Sunday, when the hour extended to 9:00 P.M. so people would be able to attend religious services. Other decrees soon followed. One that forbade farm produce from the neighboring countryside to be brought into town drew the largest outcry.[3]

Milroy's actions had their intended effect. Food, already hard for citizens to obtain, became even more so. "The reins are being tightened over us every day. We can buy only the barest of necessities of life," said Cornelia McDonald in January. A month later, Mrs. McDonald sent one of her boys beyond the Federal lines to contact his father and return with the funds needed to survive. "We find it so hard to live," she said. "So hard to get anything to eat."[4]

Prohibited from obtaining what they needed through legal channels, Winchester residents did not hesitate to employ alternative means. Realizing it would be in her best interests, Mrs. McDonald permitted the quartermaster of a regiment encamped on her property to use one of the rooms in her house for his quarters. Consequently, in the weeks following, he gave them provisions and wood. Her children also befriended a wagon master who passed by every day, and soon after he dropped off hay for the milk cow the family had hidden in the cellar. Although they did not have a permit to purchase items, Laura and Mary Lee used their considerable charm and wit to entice the sutlers around town into selling them whatever they wanted. In fact, so successful was Mrs. Lee in her endeavors that she wondered if they viewed her to be Northern in sentiment, a thought that seemed to mortify her.[5]

Dedicated as they were to the cause, the Lee sisters carried their actions one step further. Not content with simply taking care of their own needs, the ladies continued to purchase whatever supplies they could throughout the winter, with the intention of distributing them to the Confederate troops when they returned. To help finance their secretive operation, friends from Baltimore smuggled in funds. These resourceful ladies also employed friends to purchase items so not as to attract the attention of the Federals. Considering the restraints they worked under, their efforts proved to be highly successful. By April they had accumulated almost 100 pounds of coffee and sugar; a large quantity of molasses; a lesser amount of potatoes, beans, oil, and dried fruit; and several hundred dollars' worth of boots, shoes, and clothing. The women also took immense satisfaction in outwitting their oppressors. "It requires no little management," declared Mrs. Lee, "to spend so much money judiciously & to collect such treasonable supplies, without exciting suspicion. If Milroy knew my occupation I would be sent to Fort Deleware [sic]."[6]

Mrs. Hugh (Mary) Lee. Born in Richmond in September 1819, Mary Lee later married Hugh Holmes Lee of Winchester in May 1843. After Mr. Holmes died in 1858 Mrs. Lee remained in Winchester, and during the war she was an avid supporter of the Confederate cause. After the war Mrs. Lee moved to Baltimore where she was one of the founders of the Daughters of the Confederacy, and an officer of the Baltimore chapter until her death in 1906.

The townspeople also quickly came to abhor Milroy's practice of taking over their homes for use as living quarters or hospitals. As they had the year before, many of the higher-ranking officers established their head-quarters in private residences, usually taking over several rooms or a wing of the house. Detestable as this was, the people had by now come to accept the invasion of their privacy and homes as part of the war. But they were angered that in many instances these intrusions were totally unwarranted, their sole intent being to harass and inconvenience the residents, a charge the general readily acknowledged.[7]

But Milroy did not stop there. Aware that many citizens were involved in secreting away a wide array of contraband articles and smuggling letters to and from friends on the outside, the Federals routinely went about town searching residences. Determined to catch them, Milroy would grant individuals passes to leave town in the hope that they would be caught exiting or returning with letters or illegal items.

Milroy also refused to intervene when his troops started tearing Winchester apart. The soldiers quickly put the ax to practically every unoccupied house and building in town, carrying away stones, wood, roofing materials, and fencing for use in the construction of their quarters. This wanton destruction of the town saddened the people. Cornelia McDonald wrote of one former residence destroyed by the Yankees: "Today the walls of Mr. Mason's house were pulled over; they fell with a crash; the roof had gone long ago. The house has disappeared now, and the place which knew it will know it no more. . . . Every outbuilding is gone, the carriage house was pulled down over the carriage, crushed it of course. Nothing is left but heaps of logs which the Yankees carry away for firewood."[8]

Besieged as they were by the enemy, the Valley's inhabitants appealed to officials in Richmond for relief. In Berryville, Matthella Harrison and several neighbors wrote the government to complain about the outrages being committed throughout Clarke County. M. R. Kaufman, delegate of the General Assembly from Frederick County, after hearing about the Federals' numerous transgressions from citizens, called upon Secretary of War James Seddon to investigate the matter and see if there was a reason why the Valley's citizens were being denied military protection. What upset Kaufman the most was the current inactivity of the Confederate forces. "While I do not wish to find fault with our commanding officers," he said, "not knowing whether they are acting under orders or not, it is quite strange to me that 1,200 or 1,500 of the enemy should be allowed quietly to march into Strasburg . . . commit all sorts of thefts and atrocities, remain several days, and retire to Winchester, when we have a force in the Valley nearly double that amount of men, who upon every move of the enemy continue to fall back further and further from the enemy."[9]

Seddon referred the entire matter to Lee. Although he was not familiar with all of the facts, Lee informed the secretary that though the forces stationed in the Valley were previously deemed sufficient to defend it, the advance of winter and the inclement weather made it difficult for them to operate with any real chance of success. The Confederates also faced a shortage of provisions, which hindered their ability to field a large force or sustain an advance against the enemy. He also stated that the Federals' superiority in numbers made it impossible for the Confederates to protect every point from Federal incursions. Lee would have sent reinforcements if available, but none were, and all he could tell the secretary was "I fear we can afford but little protection to the Valley District this winter."[10]

Also disquieting to Lee was the inability to secure adequate provisions for his army. On January 23, 1863, he told President Davis: "The want of supplies for the troops . . . causes me the greatest uneasiness. Unless regular supplies can be obtained, I fear the efficiency of the army will be reduced by many thousand men, when already the army is far inferior in numbers to that of the enemy." Three days later, he informed Seddon that the army had only one week's reserve of beef and salt meat available for the men; once that supply was consumed, he did not know where future supplies would come from. "The question of provisioning the army is becoming one of greater difficulty every day," he said, cautioning Seddon that if proper rations were not forthcoming, it would be impossible to keep the army together.[11]

In his attempts to obtain subsistence, the Valley was one of the first places Lee turned to. On December 29, 1862, he had directed Brig. Gen. W. E. Jones, commander of the Valley District, to ascertain and report on the amount of subsistence and forage the army could expect to obtain from the region. Jones's report a month later only heightened Lee's concern. In transmitting its details to his superiors in Richmond, Lee informed the secretary of war that there were "but few cattle in the Valley," and those Jones needed for his own command. He told him that all excess bacon was being collected and forwarded to Staunton. Considering the depleted supply of hogs in Virginia, however, the amount could not have been very substantial. The only commodity that could be found in any quantity was wheat, but a shortage of wagons limited the amount that could be collected.[12]

Unable to secure enough provisions for his army in the Valley, Lee looked farther to the west. In late January he notified Jones that an expedition should be sent into Hampshire, Tucker, Randolph, Pendleton, and Highland Counties to collect cattle and bacon. This was not the only time Lee would resort to such measures. In the upcoming months, he on several occasions ordered forays into West Virginia in an effort to produce subsistence, and when he directed Jones and Brig. Gen. John D. Imboden to launch an attack on the Baltimore and

Ohio Railroad in April to disrupt Federal communication with the west, he reminded both commanders that the acquisition of supplies was as vital a part of the operation as the destruction of the railroad. "You must bear in mind," Lee told Imboden, "that the collection of horses, cattle, provision, & c., is of primary importance to us—as much so as the destruction of the railroad. I request, therefore, that nothing be neglected on your part to obtain as large a supply as possible."[13]

But these expeditions contributed little to the overall supply of the army. By now the bulk of the army's subsistence was coming from outside Virginia, and Lee began to voice concern over the efficiency of the railroads. In late January, after hearing that provisions were being held up because of a delay in the running of the freight trains, he implored President Davis to order the supplies forwarded at once. Lee made a similar plea to Seddon two weeks later: "From the reports brought by Lieutenant-Colonel Cole, chief commissary, I understand that the principal reliance for meat is based upon the present supplies at Atlanta and in Tennessee, and that the chief difficulty will be in its regular transportation by rail to Richmond. Will you allow me to suggest that energetic agents of the Quartermaster's Department be at once detailed . . . to attend to the transportation of this meat from Atlanta to Richmond." To make sure supplies were forwarded promptly, he recommended that the shipment of all nonessential articles be temporarily suspended and even offered to send troops to help repair the bridges recently destroyed by the enemy along part of the Tennessee and Virginia Railroad. Lee was still expressing his displeasure about the railroad's shortcomings in April when he discovered that a hundred carloads of supplies destined for the army had been detained in North Carolina for more than two weeks.[14]

Another concern was the deteriorating condition of the Virginia Central Railroad. It was already limited in its ability to provide transportation—in 1861 it had only 27 locomotives, 23 passenger cars, 11 mail and baggage cars, 22 coal and gravel cars, and 188 flat and boxcars—and the demands of the war quickly taxed the line beyond its capabilities. Responding to a complaint in regard to a delay in the shipment of 1,000 barrels of flour in late September 1861, Henry D. Whitcomb, general superintendent of the railroad, had told Maj. W. S. Ashe of the Quartermaster Department that the railroad simply could not accommodate all the demands of the military: "This road was provided with barely stock enough for the transportation of produce, & c., in ordinary times, and even then we had delay from the want of cars at certain seasons. Now we have the armies of the west, the Northwest, and of the Potomac, the population of a considerable city, to supply." Compounding the problem was the fact that government freight was irregular. Without any prior notice, the military would demand large quantities of supplies be shipped immediately, but because of the railroad's limited means, this was impossible to accomplish.[15]

Of still greater concern to Whitcomb was the worsening state of the equipment, in constant use since the beginning of the war. In his annual report to the stockholders in November 1861, he said: "The locomotives are constantly used with loads to the extent of their capacity, and cannot be spared repairs; they are run until they can run no longer. Many of them are old, and constantly out of order. The freight cars, also, have been in constant use. The supply of cars being limited, makes it necessary to run them without repairs as long as it is safe to do so. They have been seriously damaged in the transportation of troops and considerable expense is necessary to put them in good order."[16]

Conditions continued to deteriorate along the line throughout 1862. Service and schedules were interrupted along the entire roadway by Federal raids against the railroad during the summer months. In July they tore up several portions of the roadbed and destroyed the South Anna Bridge and the Confederate depot at Beaver Dam Creek, and in August they burned several bridges between Richmond and Gordonsville. Afraid of losing equipment, the railroad suspended service above Gordonsville for a time in July, until the government assured the company its assets would be protected. Aside from the Federal attacks, the equipment and the roadway throughout the year continued to decline in efficiency, to the point where Whitcomb in November 1862 wondered if the railroad would be able to function if the war lasted much longer.

> It is hardly to be doubted that the rapid decline in the efficiency of our roads is soon to diminish our means of successfully maintaining our struggle for independence. . . . If the speed of our trains is judiciously reduced, with reference to the deprecation of the rails, our roads will last many years longer. In conformity with these views, the speed of our trains has been much lessened, and, if necessary, will be to a greater extent.

The impact of how far the railroad's capabilities had deteriorated can be seen by early February 1863. Desperate to obtain forage for the army's horses, Lee called upon the Virginia Central to deliver 90,000 pounds a day, but the railroad never was able to deliver more than 30,000 pounds a day, and even then the shipments were erratic and irregular.[17]

By the spring of 1863, the situation had become critical. Lee had already dispersed the army in order to feed it, in February transferring several units of cavalry and a number of artillery horses to the Lower Rappahannock and south of the James River, and almost half of Longstreet's Corps was sent to Suffolk to counteract the Federal presence there and collect supplies. Lee stated that he would be unable to assume the offensive if more adequate supplies were not forthcoming on a regular basis. Lee, moreover, was depending upon the supplies collected in North Carolina to support the army when it did advance. In April he told Davis, "I had hoped by General Longstreet's operations in North Carolina to obtain sufficient subsistence to commence the movement, and by the operations in Northwestern Virginia to continue the supplies. . . . At present we are very much scattered, and I am unable to bring the army together for the want of proper subsistence and forage."

. Just as alarming to Lee was the condition of the troops. They had been on short rations since the beginning of the year and were hardly getting enough to sustain themselves. Their daily allotment consisted of a quarter pound of bacon, 18 ounces of flour, one-tenth of a pound of rice every three days, a few peas, and occasionally some molasses and dried fruit. Scurvy began to be a problem, and in an attempt to add vegetables to their diet, details were sent out to gather sassafras buds, onions, poke sprouts, and other vegetation. "This may give existence to the troops while idle," Lee commented, "but will certainly cause them to break down when called upon for exertion."[18]

The authorities in Richmond were equally concerned, and they assured the general that everything possible was being done to provide the army with proper rations, both now and in the future. Aware that the immediate problem was more one of transportation than of the scarcity of supplies, Seddon contacted Col. William M. Wadley, agent in charge of railroad transportation, in late March to see what could be done to improve the efficiency of the railroads. Harmony, cooperation, and reasonable energy, Seddon said, were required on the part of the different railroads to correct the current deficiencies. The secretary summoned the presidents of the most important railroads to a meeting in Richmond so they could confer and determine the best course of action to improve railroad transportation.[19]

Hard-pressed to keep the army supplied, and with all current measures at their disposal exhausted, the government appealed to its citizens for help. In an address to the Confederate nation on April 10, Davis called upon the people to put aside all thoughts of personal gain and forward without delay any surplus provisions to the military forces in the field. By doing so, he told them, they would be giving invaluable assistance to the army at a time when it was most needed and enhance their ability to defeat the enemy. By answering the call, they would be doing their part to help preserve the sovereignty and independence of their country.[20]

The Valley newspapers also called for the people to act without delay in forwarding supplies, and they were right in doing so. As April ended, it was only a matter of days before the Federal Army of the Potomac, under the command of Maj. Gen. Joseph Hooker, broke camp and marched south in search of Lee and the Confederate Army of Northern Virginia.

Learning that Hooker was attempting to get around his left and attack his rear, Lee turned the tables on his adversity in the tangled and wooded countryside 10 miles west of Fredericksburg. In a daring move, Lee directed Jackson to take his entire corps, over 26,000 men, beyond the Federal right flank, which was currently exposed, and launch an all-out assault. At 5:15 P.M. on May 2, the Confederate bugles rang out, and Jackson's battle-hardened veterans—three rows deep, spread out more than a mile wide, and yelling like demons—charged forward through the dense woods and thick underbrush. The Federal line, which was not expecting an attack, was taken completely off guard, and the cover of darkness was the only thing that kept them from being completely destroyed. Lee relentlessly pressed the attack for the next two days. Totally defeated, Hooker pulled his battered army back behind the Rappahannock River during the night of May 5, putting an end to the battle and the campaign.[21]

The Battle of Chancellorsville, as the engagement came to be known, was a resounding Confederate victory. But the victory, while brilliant, exacted an extremely high price: Casualties for the four-day contest totaled almost 13,000 men, among them Jackson, the one soldier the Confederacy could ill afford to lose.[22]

Jackson's death cast a pall over the entire Confederacy, but nowhere was his loss more heartfelt than in the Valley. He had been a longtime resident before the war and had received his greatest accolades in defending it the previous summer, and many Valley inhabitants loved him and had come to look upon him as their savior.

For others it was more personal. Upon hearing of his friend's demise, the Rev. Francis McFarland wrote, "The sad intelligence has reached me today of the death of my valued noble friend, Lieut. Gen. Thomas J. Jackson. It has produced a feeling of sadness & distress such as I have rarely experienced on the death of any one. It is a national Calamity of no ordinary weight." In Lexington, Margaret Preston had just finished writing a letter to the general inviting him to visit with the family, when word arrived that he was dead. "At five this evening the startling confirmation comes—Jackson is indeed dead!" she cried out. "Oh, the havoc death is making. . . . Alas! Alas! When is the end to be?" A dark cloud of despair hung over the Shenandoah, and many people began to wonder if they would ever see relief from the enemy now that the "Champion of the Valley" was no more.[23]

With the Confederate forces limited in their ability to provide protection, Federal cavalry during the early spring continued to travel about the countryside of the Lower Valley plundering its farms. In April and May the Yankees swept through the vicinity of Berryville five times.[24]

The citizens of Winchester faced even more difficult circumstances. Fed up with their brazen attitude and never-ending stream of insults, Milroy in April began exiling those who complained too loudly or flouted Federal authority. The first to be afforded such treatment were the Logans. Early in the evening of April 7, Mrs. Logan and her three daughters were taken by wagon several miles south of town, where they were left on the side of the road, bereft of their possessions and left to fend for themselves. A week later, after intercepting a letter in which she had written a detailed account of the incident to a close friend in New Jersey, as well as her own scathing opinion of it, Milroy had Mary Magill, long a thorn in the sides of the Federals, banished from the city. Over the next two months, several of Winchester's leading citizens would pay the same price for being outspoken in their criticism of Milroy or his policies.

Cut off and isolated as they were, many of Winchester's residents began to wonder if they would ever be released from their current bondage. Rumors of Confederate cavalry coming to their rescue had been circulating about town for weeks, but they never materialized, and the townspeople became skeptical of subsequent reports.

On the outskirts of town, Cornelia McDonald questioned how much longer she would be able to resist the invasions of her captors, and the thought of packing everything up and leaving for quieter surroundings was becoming more and more attractive. She had become pale and weak because of the lack of proper nourishment, and the Federals' constant intrusions and despicable behavior had pushed her nearly to the breaking point. Every time she heard footsteps on the front porch, she became frightened and wondered what hardship awaited her next. Realizing that she would be unable to combat her fears much longer, but not wanting to leave, she prayed for a quick return of the Confederates.[25]

Mrs. McDonald's prayers were soon answered. Following the Battle of Chancellorsville, General Lee and President Davis, after consultation with the cabinet, agreed upon a plan that called for a military invasion of Pennsylvania. Most important to the citizens of the Lower Valley was that the Confederate army would enter Pennsylvania by way of the Shenandoah Valley to provide its residents relief from the enemy.

Lee put his army into motion on June 3, the three corps of the army making their way toward the Blue Ridge Mountains and the Valley. Ten days later, two divisions of the 2nd Corps, led by Lt. Gen. Richard S. Ewell, were on the outskirts of Winchester, encamped in the countryside to the south, intent on giving battle. The infantry and artillery were deployed to advantage, and the Confederates attacked at 6:00 the following evening. They quickly overwhelmed the Federal garrison, routing them from their defenses. Milroy and several hundred of this cavalry managed to escape, but they were the only ones to do so. The victorious Confederates took over 4,000 prisoners and captured twenty-three pieces of artillery and some 300 wagons loaded with military stores.[25]

The day they had so long awaited was finally at hand, and Winchester's residents poured out into the streets at first light to celebrate and welcome their liberators. Mary and Laura Lee did not even wait until then. Roused by distant gunfire, they got up at 4:00 A.M. and happily greeted the first soldiers to enter the city. By 7:00 A.M. hundreds of the town's residents had assembled on Main Street, waving and cheering as the troops filed by. Laura later described the scene: "The people were perfectly wild with delight and excitement and the troops no less so." Before long, the sidewalk outside the Winchester Hotel was crowded with people celebrating the moment, laughing, singing, cheering, and giving hurrahs to the Confederacy and the ladies of Winchester. Soon after, Mary and Laura returned home and started preparing breakfast for the soldiers, a steady flow of whom stopped by for the rare treat of a home-cooked meal until well past noon. They also gave many of the articles they had secretly purchased and stored away to the soldiers, General Ewell among them.[26]

The people continued to show their appreciation the next day. In the morning, Cornelia McDonald traveled into town to assist several of her neighbors in making a Confederate flag from two captured Union ones. They later presented it to General Ewell, who had the flag raised at the Federal fortifications, renamed Fort Jackson by the people, during the planned celebration that afternoon. The Lee sisters again served breakfast and handed out clothes to those who came by, and when an adjutant of Ewell's staff appeared, Mary

invited Ewell and General Early to come to their house for tea after the cere-
monies at the fort. The two men graciously accepted, and Ewell even sent his
carriage to take the ladies to the fort. Afterward he accompanied them back to
their residence, where they sat in the front yard for over an hour sipping tea and
engaging in pleasant conversation.[27]

Although Ewell and his men enjoyed this treatment and certainly would
have liked to remain in Winchester, duty called from beyond the Potomac. Lee
had never intended to give battle at Gettysburg; the fight came about by acci-
dent. A Confederate division of infantry were there on the morning of July 1
in quest of a reported supply of shoes and ran into two brigades of Federal cavalry deployed just west of the town. Lee had told his subordinates not to bring
on a general engagement until the army, spread out north and west of town,
was united, but as soon as the two forces came in contact with each other, they
started fighting. The fighting quickly escalated, the sounds of the gunfire and
artillery drawing the troops of both armies into the fray.

Although reluctant to initiate a major battle, Lee changed his mind after
reaching the field and ordered a full-scale attack. He had good reason to do so.
The Confederate divisions were arriving on the scene faster than those of the
enemy, and when allowed to advance, they drove the Federals from Gettysburg
in confusion to the hills and ridges south of the town. Now committed to
being the aggressors, the Confederates launched a number of furious assaults
against the Federals' left the next day. They achieved partial success early on,
but in the end they failed to drive the Federals from their works along the
southern portion of Cemetery Ridge or dislodge them from their defenses on
Little Round Top.

Unable to penetrate either of their flanks, Lee on July 3 attacked the Federal center. To break through their line, he would use three divisions of
infantry, almost 15,000 men. Preceded by a two-hour artillery barrage to soften
the Federal defenses, the Confederate assault column, more than a mile wide,
came out of the woods opposite Cemetery Ridge a few minutes after 3:00 P.M.
and stepped off. Though grand in spectacle, the attack had little chance of
success. As the Confederates advanced across the mile-wide field devoid of
cover, Federal gunners with shot, shell, and canister tore huge gaps in their
lines. Then, when they were within range, Yankee infantry in front and on
both flanks poured a blistering fire into their ranks. Incredibly, about 300
Southerners broke through the Federal line, but within a few minutes, they
were either cut down or captured. Not being able to withstand this withering
fire, the Southern assault collapsed, and those still standing tried to make their

way back across the bloody field, now littered with thousands of dead and wounded. Of the 15,000 Confederates who had taken part in the charge, less than half returned.[28]

Defeated, Lee had no choice but to return to Virginia. The retreat originated on the afternoon of the fourth, with the supply train and some 12,700 wounded making their way back toward the Potomac River. When night fell, the infantry formed ranks and joined the procession. A torrential rain fell throughout the night and into the morning, making the march even more difficult and dismal. Three days later, both the wagon train and the army were before the river crossings at Williamsport, but the waters of the Potomac were extremely high and unfordable. After a week's delay, the army marched south to Bunker Hill, where they took rest in the neighboring countryside.[29]

Tired and hungry from the grueling campaign, the troops fanned out across the region in search of food. Taken aback by their numbers, one woman exclaimed: "The soldiers were swarming around us like bees. They are camped near Mr. Hanshaw's Mill, some others are in one of Uncle George's fields. They are scouring the country for provisions of every kind, for man and beast." Just outside Gerrardstown, Sarah McKown constantly prepared meals as soldiers stopped by at all hours of the day and night to get something to eat. Matthella Harrison also found her premises invaded by scores of famished Rebels wanting to be fed.[30]

Circumstances were just as chaotic in Winchester. As on a number of previous occasions, the town quickly became inundated with thousands of wounded from the battlefield. Compounding the problem was the fact that the local population had been in a terrible state of health for months, with various illnesses, including typhoid fever. Those wounded that could be moved were sent to convalesce farther up the Valley in Staunton. But this did little to relieve the overall crowding, and the town in many ways turned into one vast hospital, with soldiers quartered in just about every public building and the residents opening their doors to provide whatever aid, shelter, and comfort they could. When a lieutenant knocked on the door of the Lee household to ask where he could take two of his fellow soldiers, both of whom had just had a leg amputated, the ladies could not turn them away. They hastily prepared a section of the parlor for their lodgings, gave them a proper meal, and did their best to make their stay comfortable. To assist the civilian population in feeding the soldiers, the army commissary distributed rations for them to prepare, which they appreciated, but even so the task at hand was daunting, as the wounded were still being brought into town two weeks after the battle.[31]

The Gettysburg campaign was the most costly to date in the expenditure of human life, but the death of so many was not the only reason Valley inhabitants were downcast. The tide of the war was not going in favor of the Confederacy, as everyone well knew by the latest reverses: the defeat at Gettysburg; the loss of Vicksburg and Port Hudson on the Mississippi River, which split the Confederacy in two; the Federal advance into middle Tennessee; and the renewed attack on Charleston. Capt. Frank M. Imboden, an Augusta County native now serving with the 18th Virginia Cavalry, stationed in the Valley, wrote in his diary as July came to an end: "Another month has passed and the results are perhaps more disastrous than were Feb. '62. Vicksburg, Port Hudson, Gettysburg have been fought and leave gloom on the country. Unless changing success attends the Confederate arms, fits of despondency overhang every community." Even as staunch a secessionist as Laura Lee acknowledged that the situation was not very encouraging. "Things have a very depressing appearance for us right now," she said. "The loss of Vicksburg and Port Hudson are serious calamities."[32]

Adding to the overall feeling of despair was the fact that the Confederate military would no longer be present to protect the Valley from the Yankees. In late July, to counter the movements of the Federals and protect the Confederate capital, Lee issued orders for the army to return to a defensive position east of the Blue Ridge. With only two brigades of cavalry left behind to defend the region, many Valley inhabitants were apprehensive and feared the worst. Mary Lee had no confidence in their ability to provide protection: "Surely this Valley is doomed, since Ashby and Jackson have been taken from us." Matthella Harrison also expressed displeasure over the army leaving: "These are dark days . . . I had strongly hoped this fall would see the end of this dreadful war. Instead of that we see the army apparently on retreat and we, either left to the mercy of the Yankees or compelled to leave our homes."[33]

And leave many did. Numerous families chose to gather up their belongings and depart for quieter surroundings rather than live through another Federal occupation. So many were leaving that for a short while, just about everything that had wheels on it was in demand and exacted a high price. One of those who opted to leave was Cornelia McDonald. On July 18, she and her children left their Winchester home, to which they would never return, and after a month's journey, they settled down in Lexington, where they resided for the rest of the war.[34]

Actually, there had been an ongoing exodus from the city and other portions of the Lower Valley for months, ever since Jackson's withdrawal in

November. The majority, facing an uncertain future and with nowhere to go, migrated farther up the Valley. As a result, most of the communities to the south—Woodstock, Harrisonburg, Staunton, Lexington—became crowded with hundreds of refugees in search of food and shelter, and concerned about how they were going to survive. By summer one longtime Lexington resident said she scarcely recognized anyone she met in her travels about town.[36]

In his headquarters at Culpeper Court House, east of the Blue Ridge, Lee was concerned about the future well-being of his command. The defeat at Gettysburg had thwarted his plan of collecting supplies and feeding his men from the lush Pennsylvania countryside, and upon their return to Virginia, he once again faced the problem of provisioning the army.

In trying to accomplish that goal, Lee quickly discovered that he would have to look elsewhere besides the Valley. During the army's short stay there, men and teams had been sent out to collect supplies but for the most part came back empty-handed; cattle were few, and there was little grain or flour to be found. To furnish the troops with suitable rations, he had to use captured beef brought back from Pennsylvania. Lee did not give up on the Valley, however. In the months to come, he continued to direct his subordinates to garner all possible supplies from the region, but in spite of their best efforts, they were largely unsuccessful.[37]

Valley farms had been operating under a sever shortage of manpower from the start of the war, and since the draft had been instituted, there were not enough hands left at home to work the land in a productive manner. Furthermore, there were few slaves, as thousands had taken flight during the first two years of the war. In many cases, the only ones left to work the farms were women and young children. In early May Marcus Buck told his son Richard, "A great effort is being made here now to raise crops of Corn, Oats, & c, but the prospect is gloomy indeed, with but little horses and hand power left, and with the prospect of being constantly interfered in its cultivation and forceably losing hand, horses, and crops." After leaving the Valley in late July, Lee reported to President Davis that "while there, in order to obtain sufficient flour, we were obliged to send men and horses [into the fields to] thresh the wheat, carry it to the mills, and have it ground." As Winchester resident Kate McDonald and her family traveled up the Valley following their departure from their home, she observed that "no fields were planted, no farming going on in the richest place of ground in the world."

The farmers' plight, moreover, only promised to get worse. To augment the nation's dwindling military forces, the Confederate Congress later in the year tightened several provisions of the draft and began to consider expanding the age limits in both directions. Aware of what was going on in Richmond, James D. Davidson in Lexington notified the governor that he opposed the measure, knowing full well the adverse effect it would have on agriculture. "Bread and meat are now more important to the army than men," he told Letcher. "Call out all as is proposed & the desolation of farms will be like that of the threat of the enemy."[38]

Another problem was the lack of horses. By this time, farmers had been deprived of substantial numbers of their workhorses, inhibiting or preventing altogether the tilling of fields and the planting and harvesting of crops. The farmers could not replace their losses by falling back on other work animals. In cultivating their land, they relied almost exclusively on horses to plow the fields and perform all the heavy labor. When the fighting erupted in 1861, there were fewer than 2,300 mules and oxen in use throughout the region.

The Federals were partly to blame for this shortfall, particularly in the four counties of the Lower Valley, but the Confederate military was even more responsible. Since the start of the war, the cavalry and artillery units were in constant need of horses due to battlefield losses, and the Valley was one of the first places they looked for replacements. James Davidson, of Lexington, had all of his horses commandeered by the army as early as September 1861, though most farmers did not actually begin to feel the pinch until spring of the following year. Early in March 1862, William Hooke, of Augusta County, told his son, "The last requisition made for horses only leaves 2 horses on the farm, unless to those farming very large and working a good many hands, so it will be a hard matter to get out a spring crop." Rather than lose their horses to the enemy or their own forces, a number of individuals sold them, as they were currently demanding a high price at auctions and from speculators.[39]

By 1863 horses were being stolen by both sides. "Robberies are becoming of frequent occurrence in this part of the Valley. . . . Horse stealing has become exceedingly common," the *Rockingham Register* reported in June. This practice continued almost unabated until the war's end, due in part to military regulations. Unlike their Federal counterparts, Confederate troopers were personally responsible for providing their own mounts. If an animal went lame, was wounded in battle, or became disabled in any other way, it was up to the cavalryman, not the army, to secure a replacement. If unable, the soldier after a time faced the prospect of being transferred to infantry, a circumstance he most fervently hoped to avoid.[40]

Then there was the weather. After suffering through the severe drought of the previous year, farmers in the summer of 1863 had to contend with excessive rain, which considerably delayed farming operations and damaged most of the year's wheat harvest, negating any chance of the army's accumulating a reserve supply.[41]

There was yet another reason why ample supplies could no longer be found in the Valley. Angered over and unwillingly to put up with their produce being impressed by the army or government agents for prices far below market value, many farmers by 1863 had begun to withhold supplies and work only enough land to suit their own purposes. When agents in January began impressing corn in Rockbridge County for almost 50 percent less than the current price, the *Lexington Gazette* called it an act of tyranny and oppression on the part of the government. The *Staunton Spectator* in early March voiced objection to the injustice being done to the farmers and warned what would happen if the authorities in Richmond did not intervene:

> We understand that the military officers have been impressing grain, meat, & c, of the farmers of this county, and have been allowing them prices greatly below the market value. We do not know that there is any legal authority for such impressments as we know of no provision having been made by Congress. . . . We do not believe that persons should be allowed to hoard a surplus of supplies when they are needed for the subsistence of our army, nor do we believe that they should be taken from the owner without allowing him the local market value of them. . . . Let the Government adopt this policy, and there would be no necessity to resort to impressment, except to those who hoard their products. . . . If the farmers shall have a guarantee that the fruits of their hard labor will not be taken from them at less than a fair compensation they will cultivate as much land as possible, but if they are to be subject to impressments which will not allow half price for their products, they will not cultivate more land than is necessary to supply their own families.[42]

Responding to the host of complaints, Congress passed legislation on March 26, 1863, to regulate impressment and curb its many abuses. The bill, which came to be known as the impressment act, called for the creation of a commission that would establish fair prices and act as an arbitrator whenever a dispute arose between agent and farmer over just compensation. Though sound in theory, the law did little to alleviate the problem. When setting prices, the commission routinely failed to take into account the skyrocketing rate of inflation, which made most of the prices obsolete before they even took effect. As a result, there was a huge discrepancy between what the government and the farmer considered to be the fair market price for nearly every item.

A second piece of legislation enacted by the government on April 24 drew an even larger outcry from the farmers. Desperate to keep the army supplied, Congress sanctioned a bill that placed a tax on all agricultural produce, called the tax-in-kind act. The act required all farmers, after putting aside enough for their own needs, to give 10 percent of their harvest of all products to the government.[43]

Intended to cure major ills, the two measures instead only intensified the farmers' overall feeling of discontent. They felt that they were being called upon to carry the lion's share in supporting the war, while other classes sacrificed little. As one senior-ranking Commissary Department official sadly noted, the policy of impressment and the arbitrary manner in which it was enforced had "taxed the patriotism, liberality, and means of the people to the utmost limit of endurance." That it had, to the point where many farmers had become indifferent, if not openly hostile, toward the Confederate cause, which they demonstrated by withholding their support. Throughout the following months, an increasing number of Valley farmers withheld meat, bacon, and grain from commissary and tax-in-kind agents; left substantial tracts of their land fallow; opted to sell any excess produce to speculators; and refused to furnish anything to the government except what was impressed.

A longtime opponent of impressment, the *Staunton Spectator* in late October 1863 chastised the government for continuing to adhere to such a policy. "In this crisis of our affairs," the paper wrote, "the policy of our government should be directed to stimulate productions, and to diminish consumption. But by some strange infatuation, our officials act as if they were influenced by an exact opposite purpose. The administration of the impressment law tends to directly . . . repress productions. No man knows when he sows his crop whether he will be allowed to reap and market it. . . . This system of mal-administration disadvantages the farmer, and tends directly to diminish productions."

And James D. Davidson commented on the debilitating effects of the government's policy in a letter to a longtime friend, Col. Samuel Reid:

> I find that the system of impressments is a source of such dissatisfaction
> and complaint, and that many farmers say they will not plant more

than will serve their own wants. The system is wrong in many respects and works unjustly and unequally on the farmer. Our people are willing to bear any amount of taxation, provided it falls uniformly on all. But when a farmer is forced to sell his flour at $25.00, to pay fabulous prices for everything he cannot make himself, he has part cause to say what is the justice of binding him down to fixed prices and allowing others to exact *ad libitum,* for every thing we are compelled to buy from them. From what I have seen, I am satisfied that the system of impressments is demoralizing our best people, not because the government adopts it, but on account of the manner of its execution and the irregularity and harshness of its operation on selected classes.[44]

All of the above factors collectively were responsible for the extreme decline in crop production throughout the Valley. Just how much of an effect they had can be ascertained by examining several tax-in-kind estimates for 1863. Although the tax-in-kind records for the ten counties of the Shenandoah Valley cannot be found, the 1863 estimates for five counties adjacent to the Valley—Albemarle, Amherst, Buckingham, Fluvanna, and Nelson—have survived (see map on page 152), and from them an approximation of each county's harvest in wheat, corn, and oats can be calculated. If the crop estimates for these five counties are compared with those of the 1860 agricultural census, a fairly accurate judgment can be made of the war's effect on grain production throughout northern Virginia. The following tables compare the 1863 crop yield estimates of wheat, corn, and oats with the yields of 1860.

WHEAT PRODUCTION
(In Bushels)

	1860	1863 Estimate	% Change
Albemarle	302,307	87,315	–71.2%
Amherst	104,111	50,091	–51.9%
Buckingham	114,921	52,427	–54.4%
Fluvanna	127,704	94,667	–26.0%
Nelson	78,306	57,290	–26.9%
Totals	**727,349**	**341,790**	**–53.0%**

CORN PRODUCTION
(In Bushels)

	1860	1863 Estimate	% Change
Albemarle	729,710	441,649	-70.3%
Amherst	313,809	137,677	-56.1%
Buckingham	—	—	—
Fluvanna	210,287	127,419	-39.5%
Nelson	339,075	233,870	-31.1%
Totals	1,592,881	940,615	-41.0%

OAT PRODUCTION
(In Bushels)

	1860	1863 Estimate	% Change
Albemarle	215,273	63,956	-70.3%
Amherst	120,047	38,274	-68.2%
Buckingham	178,132	46,614	-74.9%
Fluvanna	97,586	41,548	-57.5%
Nelson	91,646	25,725	-72.0%
Totals	702,684	216,117	-69.3%

As the tables clearly illustrate, the war had a devastating impact on grain production in the five counties. Even taking into account the likelihood that the farmers intentionally underestimated their harvests, the totals are exceedingly small. But of greater significance, the findings support the contention that a corresponding decline in productivity occurred in the Valley, which was one of the major battlegrounds of the war in Virginia, whereas no major battle or campaign ever occurred in the five counties east of the Blue Ridge. If a region that saw no conflict suffered 40 to 70 percent declines in overall grain production, it is likely that Valley farmers experienced equal, if not greater, losses.[45]

A number of Commissary Department records also confirm the extent to which agriculture in the Valley and the rest of Virginia had been depleted. Submitting a report to the War Department, an official from the tax-in-kind bureau stated that during the five-month period between July and November, agents were able to collect only 62,461 bushels of wheat, 36,417 bushels of corn, 19,720 bushels of oats, and 1,486,822 pounds of hay from all the territory in Virginia still under the control of the Confederacy. Adding to the bleak picture, Maj. B. P. Noland, chief commissary for the state of Virginia, informed his superiors in November that his officers had purchased almost nothing during the previous month because farmers were instead selling to speculators who were offering double the price.

As for beef, the situation was worse. In his annual report to the secretary of war, Commissary General Northrop stated that as of October 15, the total number of cattle available in the Valley and the rest of Virginia east of the Blue Ridge did not exceed 6,000. Two months later, another of Northrop's assistants, Maj. S. B. French, notified him that the Commissary Department in all of the states east of the Mississippi River had on hand only a twenty-five-day supply of meat for 400,000 men. In closing, he emphasized, "It is again presented with the remark that the meat ration is nearly exhausted in Virginia, the last pound here having been forwarded to General Lee's army, and there is no 'reserve depot' to draw upon."[46]

With food in short supply, Valley inhabitants viewed the coming months with trepidation. Compounding the woes of the average citizen was the burgeoning rate of inflation. In the three months after Gettysburg and Vicksburg, prices rose almost 60 percent. As James Davidson, of Lexington, put it, "Prices are going up & the currency going down everyday." Having lost their faith in paper money, the citizens in the country outside Winchester by August started to demand gold for their wood. Less than two months later, a barrel of flour cost $50 or more; a pound of butter, over $3; and a pound of fresh pork, almost $2.[47]

In the east, the Federals continued to pressure the Army of Northern Virginia, and in the west, after their victory at Missionary Ridge, they were readying to strike into Georgia and the heart of the Confederacy. Pondering his country's fate, Alexander H. H. Stuart shortly before Christmas told James Davidson in confidence, "Things look to me not very encouraging & I sincerely wish we were under some good & stable government, even if it had a smaller infusion of democracy in it."[48]

The war was becoming more desperate in the Valley as well. Following the Confederate withdrawal in late July, the Lower Valley for the most part had become a no-man's-land; cavalry raids by both sides were now so regular that they elicited little protest from the supporters of either flag. Even more troubling were Federal incursions to the south. Advancing from the west, Yankee cavalry early in November began to threaten Rockbridge and Augusta Counties, and the home guards of both were called out to help repel the invaders.[49]

Exposed to the war's harsh realities for almost three years, the inhabitants of the Valley had suffered severely, decidedly more than most, and they longed more than anything for an end to the fighting.

CHAPTER 6

"There Is Not Sufficient in the Valley to Live off the Country"

1864

For many, the upcoming winter would be a hard one. Unable any longer to fend for themselves, an increasing and alarming number of Valley residents were now having to depend upon the charity of others for their sur-vival. One of Lexington's more prominent and prosperous families, the Prestons, had a steady stream of visitors stopping by looking for a handout. "Poor people, soldiers' wives, & c., coming every day for flour and wood," wrote Mrs. Preston in January. "Mr. P. supplies very many of them." The Buck residence in Front Royal was also swamped with individuals in search of food. "We are having a great crowd every day & night," Marcus told his son in late February, "as *we still have something to eat.*" He wrote to his son again in April: "The house is crowded with people who can not find something to eat elsewhere."[1]

Adding to the hardship and sense of pessimism was the deplorable state of the Confederate currency. Never very stable to begin with, it had by now become practically worthless. "It costs us a great deal to live now, the currency has depreciated so much," Jedediah Hotchkiss told his brother. "I only look forward to the day when it shall become worthless, then there will be an improvement. . . . My neighbors kindly sold me provisions at government prices, or I should not have been able to support my family."

In an effort to curb the rampant inflation, Congress passed legislation in February that called for the currency to be devalued by one-third starting April 1. But instead of stabilizing the economy and lowering prices, the measure precipitated the exact opposite. Afraid of being stuck with worthless notes when the law took effect, many individuals dumped them the first chance they had, flooding the market even more; others refused to accept Confederate money altogether, opting instead to barter with customers for their products or services. One Valley shoemaker, for example, refused to make a pair of shoes for a customer unless she sent him a load of wood.

The act also set off another round of astronomical price increases. Flour, which had already climbed to $125 a barrel, doubled in price almost overnight. A bushel of corn now sold for $15; a gallon of molasses, $30; a pound of coffee, $16; and a pound of tea, $40. Prices were just as outrageous when it came to clothing. Calico cost $12 per yard, coarse unbleached cotton went for $8, and a person would have to spend $40 for a good pair of pants.[2]

Because of military needs, the shortages and high prices were about to become even worse. Desperate to fill the ranks, Congress in February tightened several provisions of the conscription law and expanded the age limits of the draft to include seventeen-year-olds and all those between forty-five and fifty. The government's action set off a firestorm of protest. If many of those still at home were compelled to enter the army, the *Lexington Gazette* said, "Our farming interests would suffer greatly. Many, if not most farms would remain idle and go to waste. . . . Certain are we that but little would be produced for the army." Knowing full well the consequences, the *Rockingham Register* issued an even more sharply worded commentary:

> The cry in the army and out of the army is "more food!" and it behooves our representative bodies to encourage in every way, the production of every article necessary in subsistence. From what we have observed and know, there is an alarming scarcity of labor in the country even now, and if those engaged in the cultivation of the soil either by their own labor or the supervision of others are taken from their occupation, a more deadly foe than the Yankees will thin the ranks of our armies and bring death to the door of the "loved ones at home" in the next campaign. If we do not produce, we must starve, and if all the labor is put in ranks, it will not only decrease the rations of those now on half rations, but will prevent an accumulation of future stores for consumption. . . . If we believed, for one moment, that our cause could be advanced by sending every man to the field, we would say go; but it is, we know, better for the government, better for our safety, better for the citizens at home, better for the soldier in the army, that our farms should be tilled and our harvests sufficiently abundant to prevent want of the necessities of life.[3]

Anxious to avoid military service, thousands of individuals, as was their right under the law, filed petitions with enrolling officers in hopes of gaining an exemption; others petitioned various government officials or called upon several of the Valley's more influential citizens to intercede on their behalf. In March a number of Shenandoah County farmers banded together and sent a joint petition to the local conscript bureau, which forwarded it to Richmond, where it eventually landed on the desk of President Davis. They asked that all males covered by the expanded age limits in the vicinity of the enemy's lines be allowed to remain home to raise provisions for the community.[4]

John T. Harris and James D. Davidson, two of the Valley's most prominent and respected leaders, were bombarded with requests for assistance. Most individuals asserted that they were not attempting to avoid doing their part in the defense of their country but could better serve the cause by being allowed to stay on their farms and raise crops for the army. The case of Frank Moyers, alone on his farm with a wife and three young children to support, was representative of many. Isaac C. Moore, a close friend speaking on his behalf, told Davidson that if Moyers remained on his farm, he would be able to provide the army with close to 350 bushels of wheat and over 700 bushels of corn. Considering the army's need for supplies, he said this would be far more beneficial to the Confederacy than anything he could do in the army.[5]

In the Lower Valley, hostilities between Unionists and Confederates were renewed. Always simmering just below the surface, tensions flared in mid-January following the arrest of William Dooley, a Winchester Unionist who was taken into custody while attending church services. It was later discovered that several secessionist ladies were behind his arrest. Outraged, the man's son went to Martinsburg to protest and make the case known to the Federal authorities. In retaliation, the Yankees declared that if Dooley was not released within two weeks, the mayor and fifty secessionists would be taken as hostages. To show that they were serious, a squad of cavalry traveled to Winchester a couple days later and arrested Robert Conrad and another leading citizen and carried them off to Martinsburg.[6]

But the Federal response, instead of helping, only made the situation worse for the Unionists. Afraid they would be arrested and taken away by the Confederates at any moment, many of the Union men about town made preparations to leave; others did what they could to get those arrested by the Yankees released, hoping it would placate the secessionists and defuse the situation. Their fears increased even more when the home of one Union family was shot up by a group of Confederate raiders.[7]

Public morale was in decline, a number of people believing that the Valley would have to be relinquished by summer. The newspapers did their best to raise public confidence by proclaiming that circumstances were not as dour as many seemed to believe. The *Staunton Spectator* said that the result of the war would not be determined by numbers or bravery so much as by fortitude and persistent determination. The *Lexington Gazette* stated that despite the recent setbacks, the army's spirits remained high, and if everyone continued to hold true to the cause, there could be no doubt as to the final outcome. The paper also maintained that even though food was in short supply, everyone would be able to get by if they were willing to replace the meat in their diet with garden vegetables. "With a good garden, a family can be supported with little or nothing else. We believe that the poor, especially, cannot better provide against want than by giving all the attention they can to their garden."[8]

As 1864 began, the Army of Northern Virginia also faced a grim future when it came to subsistence, a subject that was of primary concern to their commanding general. "A regular supply of provisions to the troops in this army is a matter of great importance," Lee told the secretary of war in late January. "Short rations are having a bad effect upon the men, both morally and physically. . . . Unless there is a change, I fear the army cannot be kept effective, and probably cannot be kept together."[9]

Provisions sufficient to meet the demands of the army could no longer be found in any part of Virginia still under their control, and the Confederate authorities had no other recourse but to seek subsistence from beyond their borders. Using gold or Federal greenbacks, officers of the Commissary Department throughout the winter scoured the countryside north and west of their lines in search of supplies, especially beef cattle. Lee also initiated a number of similar expeditions into West Virginia. They were largely successful in their efforts, and most of the beef consumed by the army in December and January had been thus obtained. But Lee realized that these raids, while of immediate assistance, were not a long-term solution to the army's supply problem. Commissary Major Frank G. Ruffin agreed. Even if the department had the excess capital on hand to continue such purchases, which it did not, he said, it would not be long before the enemy noticed and put an immediate halt to their actions.[10]

The fact that measurable amounts of subsistence were not to be found in the Valley did not surprise Lee. At present, the troops stationed there were having a difficult time keeping themselves supplied, let alone finding excess quantities for the army. On a scouting expedition in the Lower Valley in late

January, cavalry commander Thomas Rosser informed Jubal Early, then Valley commander, that there were not many cattle to be found, and even then it would take considerable time and effort to bring them out. A couple weeks later, when Gen. John Imboden received orders to move his troops, currently encamped just outside of Lexington, farther north, he reminded his superiors that he would be hard-pressed to support his command once it left Rockbridge County:

> Until Thomas' and Walker's brigades actually move from Rockingham, I presume there is no necessity for me to move the main body of my command to that county. . . . I shall be compelled after I go to Rockingham to haul most of my grain from this [Rockbridge] county. . . . I scarcely see how it will be possible for me to subsist my horses in Rockingham when compelled to go there. . . . You are doubtless aware of the fact that Rockingham is nearly exhausted of forage and grain of all kinds, and that Shenandoah and the country below is so completely exhausted that it is with great difficulty and labor, and the constant controversies with the people, that even a small picket force can be supplied.[11]

By March the situation had become so acute that Imboden issued a public appeal for assistance in the newspapers. It was vital, he said, for the troops to be adequately supplied if they were to protect the people and their homes from the ravages of the enemy. That the citizens would provide enough rations for the men he did not doubt, but it was just as essential that the horses be fed, and he cautioned that if feed for the animals was not forthcoming, he would have no recourse but to impress what he needed. Imboden was reluctant to enact such a policy, however, because he realized it would only increase the resentment and hostility already felt toward the military.

The longtime Valley commander was not wrong in his assumption. Exasperated by the never-ending requests for supplies, the *Lexington Gazette* early in April blasted those responsible, maintaining that the point had finally been reached where enough was enough: "The people of Richmond, as well as the Confederate Government, seem to think that Rockbridge county is an inexhaustible store-house of provisions. . . . Quartermasters and Commissary agents, with all sorts of 'impressing' officers, have ranged up and down the country . . . in search of corn, flour, potatoes, bacon, beef, and cabbage. . . . The consequence has been that almost every corncrib and wheat garner in the county has been gouged to the lowest limit that would keep the owner's family and horses above starvation, and the non-producing poor of this county can see scarcely a hope of escaping actual famine." The following week, the paper chastised the local cavalry for taking the little surplus left that the county authorities had set aside for the families of soldiers and the poor. "While the army must be fed and sustained, it is equally certain that the people at home must be cared for. The aged, the women, the children, the servants and the stock must be sustained likewise."[12]

Correspondence of the Subsistence and Quartermaster Departments also shows that the Army of Northern Virginia was not receiving substantial foodstuffs from the Valley, or any other part of Virginia. On January 3 Maj. Seth B. French notified Northrop that there was no longer any bread in Richmond. "I regret to inform you that the entire stock of breadstuffs in this city has been exhausted, and we are now unable to respond to requisitions from General Lee's army. The reserve of flour and hard bread has been consumed, and the receipts of corn for the past week have been totally inadequate to our daily wants." In early February Francis Ruffin notified the secretary of war that nearly all corn for the army was now being obtained outside Virginia. French wrote to Northrop in February that the department had on hand only two days' rations for the army, with no prospect of accumulating any further supplies in all of Virginia. It would be impossible, he said, for the army to initiate any forward movements in the spring under the present circumstances. Northrop confirmed his subordinates' findings in a dispatch to Lee a month later, telling the general that the troops in Virginia depend on corn from Georgia for bread. Quartermaster General Alexander Lawton, conversing with Gen. James Longstreet about the problem of supply, said: "Last year at this time, no corn was brought to Virginia from any point beyond North Carolina, and the army was subsisted on wheat flour. Now nearly all the corn used for the horses is brought from Georgia, and the Subsistence Department has consumed all the flour and relies upon corn to be ground up into meal for the bread of the army." The records of Wells J. Hawks, chief commissary officer of the 2nd Corps, also reflected the change in the composition of the bread. Previously, Hawks had received only sporadic shipments of cornmeal, but in February and March 1864 alone he received over 1.8 million bushels of cornmeal to sustain the men.[13]

Quartermaster General Lawton also voiced reservations to Lee about the difficulties he faced in keeping the army supplied. In February he told him,

"The calls now made on us for corn by the commissary department constitute a new drain upon our limited stock. Never before has meal formed the chief ingredient of bread for your army. The recent movements of troops in North Carolina has [*sic*] interfered seriously with transportation." On March 21 he sent Lee another dispatch assuring the general that despite the problems with the railroads, he was doing everything possible to forward provisions to the troops:

> Appreciating fully the great importance and extreme difficulty of sup-plying the Army with food and forage, I have spared no efforts to have them promptly transported from the far South, now our almost sole reliance. . . . I beg you to remember, general, that up to this time last year not a car-load of corn nor subsistence stores had been brought from points beyond Raleigh for your army. Now we are feeding the soldiers and horses of that army to a great extent from Georgia.

And in April Lawton confided to yet another officer that the department was now "feeding everything in and around Richmond, and all of General Lee's army (about to be increased by Longstreet's command), with the products of South Carolina and Georgia, and the problem we are trying to solve can scarcely be contemplated without alarm." [14]

Lawton had good reason to be concerned. After three years of warfare, the Confederacy's rapidly deteriorating railroads had made his job almost impossi-ble. By now the main trunk lines could not transport the supplies the army needed, even when all private travel had been suspended. Throughout the win-ter, while Lee's army nearly starved, carloads of supplies sat in depots to the south. The inefficiency and worsening condition of the railroads also made it impossible for the government to build up a reserve supply. "We are now dependant [*sic*] on the south for bread," an officer told Northrop in February, "yet under the most favorable circumstances, with existing arrangements, it is impossible to provide for the daily wants of General Lee's army and the troops in this state, to say nothing of . . . creating a reserve in anticipation of the many emergencies likely to arise . . . from accidents on a line . . . between 600 and 700 miles in length. . . . With no efforts to improve our facilities of transporta-tion, and whilst the present defective system continues, we must remain in a condition of uncertainty that sooner or later will culminate in disaster." Ruffin had the same fears, and he told the secretary of war that practically all of the subsistence for the Army of Northern Virginia depended on the integrity of the railroad from Weldon to Petersburg; if the line was disabled or cut, disaster would ensue.[15]

Conditions on the Virginia Central Railroad were just as bad, if not worse. It was the last link in the chain of keeping his army supplied, and Lee always made certain to remind his superiors of its importance and the consequences if it should fail. Aware of its many deficiencies, one of the most glaring being the condition of the roadbed, Lee in March 1863 had called upon Seddon to assign slaves to work on the line. If it was not done, he said, the line would certainly fail later in the year, when the army would need it most. Edmund Fontaine, president of the Virginia Central Railroad, agreed with Lee's assessment, telling President Davis in a detailed letter the same month that the road's dreadful condition was seriously hampering the rail lines' ability to service the Confederacy. In one five-day period in March alone, he said, there were four derailments because of the track. Along certain portions of the line, because of rotted crossties, the ashpans of the engines pressed down into the mud. The trains were compelled to run at reduced speeds, and even then there were frequent derailments and accidents that caused countless delays in the shipment of food and forage.

But there was little anyone could do to improve the situation. At the start of the year, the government had appropriated half of the company's surplus stock of rails, never very large to begin with, to use in the construction of the line between Danville, Virginia, and Greensboro, North Carolina, preventing them from making many of the needed repairs. Crossties were also in short supply. In August 1863 P. V. Daniel, president of the Richmond, Fredericksburg, and Potomac Railroad, notified the secretary of war that much of the repair equipment of both his railroad and the Virginia Central had been ruined because of overwork. "The severe and constant use of that machinery," he said, "with little or no opportunity for repairs, greatly deteriorated and disabled it, and has since made some of it . . . permanently useless." On top of that, Federal cavalry during the spring and summer continued to wreak havoc along major portions of the line. In May they raided Louisa Court House, on the upper end of the line, and soon after, they destroyed a number of bridges east of Taylorsville, which forced the Virginia Central to use the tracks of the Richmond, Fredericksburg, and Potomac until July 25.

With the railroad about on the verge of collapse, Lee in November pleaded with the secretary of war to have the line repaired: "The condition of the Virginia Central railroad, on which we depend almost entirely for our supplies, seems to become worse everyday. I hope . . . something may be done to put it in good repair, so that it can be relied upon for the regular transportation of our supplies. If this cannot be done, the only alternative will be to fall back nearer to Richmond." So inadequate were its capabilities that by year's end, the railroad lacked the ability of handling simultaneously the transportation of both troops and supplies.[16]

The situation did not improve, and in January 1864 Lee lodged another complaint about the inefficiency of the line. "The road is now barely able to furnish limited transportation," he told Seddon. "If this is diminished it will be impossible for me to keep the army in its present position." By April circumstances had deteriorated to the point where he informed the president that any disaster along the line would compel the army to retreat into North Carolina. The Federals, realizing how vital the track was to keeping Lee's army supplied, continued to launch raids against the line. In February Gen. Hugh Kilpatrick and Col. Uric Dahlgren destroyed considerable segments of the line. In May General Sheridan led a cavalry assault south toward Richmond, where his forces destroyed the Beaver Dam Creek supply depot, several miles of track, two engines, and twenty-five freight cars. In June Gen. David Hunter advanced up the Valley, reaching Staunton on the fifth, where he destroyed the railroad station, six miles of track, and twelve bridges to the east, which kept the line closed to all traffic until after the first week of July.

But the most pressing concern at this time was the condition of the engines and train cars. On May 8, 1864, Superintendent Whitcomb notified Seddon that the railroad had only ten locomotives and 108 cars still in operation to work the entire line. Six days later, in the aftermath of Sheridan's raid of the fourteenth, the numbers fell to eight engines and 79 cars, most of which were about to fall apart due to lack of repairs. The entire railroad was on the verge of collapse.[17]

⤐┈✦┉●┉✦┈⤏

With the commencement of active operation in May 1864, most of northern Virginia once again became the scene of continuous military action. The overall Federal strategic plan called for a simultaneous three-pronged attack against the Confederate forces operating in the state. From the north, Lt. Gen. Ulysses S. Grant would direct the Army of the Potomac in its advance against Lee and the Army of Northern Virginia, currently situated in the countryside west of Fredericksburg. In the east, the Army of the James, commanded by Maj. Gen. Benjamin Butler, would threaten Richmond by advancing against the city of

Petersburg, an important railroad center vital to the defense of the Confederate capital. A third army, under the command of Maj. Gen. Franz Sigel, would
march up the Valley, destroying all crops and anything else that would be of use
to the enemy. After reaching Staunton, Grant wanted the Federal army to
destroy the Virginia Central Railroad, thereby cutting off the flow of supplies
he believed Lee was still receiving from the region. That goal accomplished,
Sigel was expected to move east of the Blue Ridge Mountains, lay waste to the
Confederate supply bases at Gordonsville and Charlottesville, and then join
forces with the Army of the Potomac outside of Richmond.[18]

In the weeks prior to the start of the campaign, Sigel marshaled his forces
in the vicinity of Martinsburg. After everything was in place, he moved forward,
taking possession of Winchester on May 1, 1864. Though in command of the
town for little more than a week, Sigel nevertheless made a lasting impression
upon its residents. Immediately upon his arrival, he forbade all talk of politics,
blocked off numerous streets to civilian traffic, and authorized wholesale
searches of residences throughout the city. Even more disturbing was his directive prohibiting supplies from being brought in from the countryside, which,
according to one individual, nearly put the town into a state of starvation.[19]

But the Federals did not remain long. On May 9 they left Winchester, the
campaign beginning with Sigel at the head of his troops as they made their way
south along the Valley Pike. The Confederates had no significant infantry stationed in the region, and they quickly assembled a makeshift force of some
5,000 men under the command of Maj. Gen. John C. Breckenridge to contest
the advance. Included were Breckenridge's two veteran brigades, about 2,500
men; Imboden's brigade of cavalry; a few other minor detachments on duty in
the Upper Valley; and all the reserve and home guard units of Augusta and
Rockbridge Counties. Desperate to put troops in the field, the Confederates
even prevailed upon the 247-man corps of cadets from the Virginia Military
Institute in Lexington.

Sigel's march up the Valley proceeded smoothly until he reached New
Market, about 60 miles from Winchester, on May 15. There, the outnumbered
Confederates attacked the Federal advance guard and drove it back. After
shelling the supporting infantry regiments with artillery, the entire command
charged forward and swept the Yankees from the field. When it was over, the
Confederates had captured six pieces of artillery and a substantial number of
prisoners, but even more important, they had forced the Federals to make a
hasty retreat back down the Valley. Sigel did not stop until he reached Strasburg, 25 miles distant.[20]

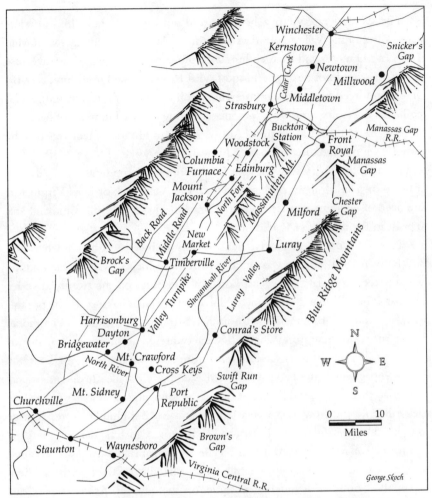

The theater of operations of the Federal Shenandoah Valley Campaign of 1864.

The Confederate victory was met with a resounding chorus of shouts and cheers from the Valley inhabitants. The cadets from the Virginia Military Institute were also jubilant. Derided by the soldiers in the days before, the cadets performed admirably during the battle, charging and capturing a key artillery position at the height of the contest. Sustaining casualties of more than 20 percent, with eight killed and forty-six wounded, the young men by their brave actions gained the respect of their fellow soldiers and were from then on spoken of highly, and to this day the anniversary of the battle is celebrated with distinction at the Institute.[21]

The Confederate victory, however, did not deter Grant in his efforts to gain control of the Valley. Four days after the battle, he replaced Sigel with Maj. Gen. David Hunter and charged him with the same instructions. To make sure that there would not be a repetition of what had happened to his predecessor, Grant reinforced Hunter by transferring a full division of infantry and several regiments of cavalry from West Virginia, bringing the total number of his command to more than 15,000 men. Also working in Hunter's favor was that he would have no one to contest his advance. In the wake of Sigel's defeat, Lee thought that the Valley was—at least for the immediate present—in no danger of being invaded. In light of that, and with the Army of Northern Virginia in dire need of reinforcements, he directed Breckinridge to take his command east to assist in the defense of Richmond.

This was Hunter's first active field command since being wounded at first Bull Run in 1861, and he was anxious to achieve success. Upon reaching his headquarters at Cedar Creek, just north of Strasburg, on the twenty-first, he designated his command the Army of the Shenandoah. The next day he put the army into motion. By June 5 the troops had marched as far south as Piedmont, 5 miles north of Staunton, where they encountered an inferior Confederate force that had just been rushed forward from southwestern Virginia. After a heated engagement, the Federals brushed aside the Confederate defenders and continued their advance, reaching Staunton the following day. Grant's orders had then called for the army to cross over the mountains, but Hunter elected instead to proceed up the Valley until he reached Lexington, which he did on June 11.[22]

In their march up the Valley, the Federals appropriated or destroyed anything that would benefit their enemies. Grant had instructed that the soldiers be supplied, and live as much as possible, off the country. At the start of the campaign, Hunter informed all brigade and lesser-grade commanders that they would be held responsible for making sure that their troops were amply supplied from the country. Horses and mules were to be seized, and all grain, cattle, hogs, and sheep were to be taken for food. They were to torch anything capable of supporting the Confederate war effort, such as flour mills, leather shops, and iron- and saltworks.

As it turned out, there was no other way for Hunter to feed his command. During the first month, only one supply train made it through to the army. All the others were attacked and looted by several bands of Confederate guerrillas that operated in the Lower Valley. The most notorious of the guerrillas was John Mosby, who by this time had gained such fame and renown for his exploits that the region in northern Virginia he presided over had come to be known as Mosby's Confederacy. The supply problem was soon felt, as rations became short and irregular, and the soldiers were quick to voice their complaints. Less than a week after starting out, Pvt. William Patterson wrote in his diary that the command was "becoming destitute of rations. How Gen. means to feed us, don't know." Frank Reader, a trooper with the 5th West Virginia Cavalry, noted that the men lived high on the hog one day and the next were reduced to half rations and scrounging about for something to eat.[23]

Although restricted by orders not to pillage and only to destroy articles deemed of military value, the troops did not hesitate to take liberty with the definitions of the two. Angered over the lack of food, the soldiers, after taking what supplies they found, often ransacked residences looking for silver, jewelry, and family valuables, or simply for revenge. It did not take much provocation for the men to reduce a place to ashes; any home that was even suspected of being used as a refuges from which to fire upon the troops as they marched by was quickly burnt to the ground.

Fearful of what the Yankees might do if they stayed, many of the remaining Upper Valley citizens chose to flee. But as one woman near Harrisonburg noted, the Yankees usually inflicted far worse damage on residences whose owners had left; those they tore to bits, breaking every piece of furniture and vandalizing the house and all of its contents.[24]

Though the Federals were indiscriminate in meting out punishment as they marched up the Valley, it nevertheless seemed that they saved the worst for Lexington. Immediately upon their arrival, they began shelling the town in the belief that the Confederate forces who had been contesting their advance remained. Over twenty houses were struck by the exploding shells, the McDonalds' and the Prestons' among them. At noon the artillery fire ceased, and the Yankee cavalry poured into the town from all directions, with the infantry on their heels. They soon began a campaign of harassment and countless acts of wanton destruction. Hungry, tired, and angry, the troops broke into scores of homes, barns, cellars, larders, icehouses, meat houses, and other buildings and took whatever they found. Within a couple of hours, hordes of soldiers swarmed over the Preston estate, and the destruction was so complete that Mr. Preston stated that $30,000 would not begin to cover his losses. Later recounting the town's destruction to a relative, another citizen wrote: "Our community has suffered greatly. Many were robbed of almost every mouthful of food and every piece of apparel."

It was clear that the Union officers were not going to put a stop to the plundering—in fact, it seemed as if they were promoting it. When two women asked Hunter to provide their homes, which were being torn apart, with protection, he scoffed at their appeal. "These are the natural consequences of war," he said, "and you must bear them as best you can."[25]

The next day the Federals began burning down many of the public buildings around the city, as well as a number of private residences. The first to be afforded such treatment were the administration buildings, military barracks, and mess hall of the Virginia Military Institute, as well as the homes of several of its professors. Next were the library and dormitories of Washington College. After that, most of the warehouses in the river district were put to the torch. After spending the night at Gov. John Letcher's home, an officer commented to one of the governor's daughters that the breakfast she was eating would probably be the last one she had in the house. He then left, and shortly after, an assistant provost marshal of Hunter's staff arrived and instructed the family to vacate the premises, as he had orders to burn it. Denied even a few minutes to gather up some clothes and a few personal belongings, Mrs. Letcher could merely watch as the troops set the house ablaze. When a neighbor reached the scene a short time later, she found Mrs. Letcher tearless and calm, but looking forlorn, as she sat in the street with her children huddled around her and the house burning in the background.

Conditioned as they were to the war, the devastation shocked and horrified even the most hardened Valley residents. From their perspective, the actions and callous behavior of the Federals far exceeded the boundaries of any kind of civilized warfare. One recipient of their depredations, Rev. William S. White of Lexington, stated, "On the whole they appeared to me like a great mob of licensed robbers and housebreakers." Twenty or so miles away in Staunton, Lucas P. Thompson was even more forthright in his condemnation. "The infamous gang of thieves, cut throats, robber bandits ought to be held up to the scorn & indignation and execration of the world. They ought if caught, every man of them to be put to the sword."[26]

With the ruins of Lexington smoldering in the distance, Hunter on June 14 proceeded to advance on Lynchburg, a vital Confederate railway and supply center located in south-central Virginia. The Confederates, however, were not about to surrender the city to the Federals. Even before Hunter took possession of Lexington, Lee foresaw that his next objective would be Lynchburg, and he immediately took steps to protect his supply base. On June 7 he dispatched Breckinridge and his command from the army at Richmond and sent him west with orders to defend the city. Realizing that additional troops would be required, Lee less than a week later sent Lt. Gen. Jubal Early and the entire II Corps of the Army of Northern Virginia, over 8,000 men, as reinforcements. Though delayed by a lack of trains, Early and a good part of his command arrived at Lynchburg five days later, just in time to contest the enemy.

Reaching the outskirts of Lynchburg on June 17, Hunter, if he had taken the initiative and attacked right away, could easily have overwhelmed the Rebel garrison and captured the city. But believing his army to be vastly outnumbered, he hesitated, opting instead to engage the enemy in a long-range artillery duel. The next morning Hunter ordered his forces to make a number of minor assaults, but they were easily driven back, and he decided not to risk any further attacks. When the Federal commander learned that Early and the II Corps had reached the field, he immediately called for the army to withdraw, which they did later that evening under the cover of darkness. Instead of retracing his steps back down the Valley, however, Hunter, citing a lack of supplies and munitions, retreated into the mountains of West Virginia. This effectively took his command out of the war for several weeks and left the Valley wide open to invasion by the Confederates.[27]

Lee wasted no time in capitalizing on his opponent's miscue. Aware that if he left the region unattended Grant would try again, he directed Early to march down the Valley and, if favorable circumstances presented themselves, to enter Maryland. Early moved quickly in carrying out his instructions. After pressing the Federal rear hard for three days, he gave his men a day's rest to catch their breath, and then proceeded with dispatch down the Valley. By July 2 the Confederates, 14,000 strong, had reached Winchester, where the general and his staff took time to have dinner and tea with a number of the ladies. Two days later the army was at Harpers Ferry. Crossing over the Potomac on the sixth, they started to march on Washington, D.C. By the eleventh they were before the environs of the city, savoring the possibility of taking the Federal capital. But after studying its defenses, and learning that two full infantry corps had arrived from Grant's army as reinforcements, Early knew he did not have the strength to capture it, and after dark the following evening, the troops began an orderly withdrawal back to Virginia.[28]

Crossing over the Potomac at White's Ford, opposite Leesburg east of the mountains, the Confederates by the sixteenth had traversed the Blue Ridge and reestablished their presence near Winchester. From there, in a little more than a week, they twice engaged the Federals. The more serious of the two encounters took place on the twenty-fourth on the old battlefield of Kernstown.

Routing the enemy from the field and capturing almost 500 prisoners, Early followed up the victory by moving his command to Martinsburg, where he gave his troops a well-deserved rest. Five days later, upon hearing that during his advance on Washington, the Yankees had burnt the homes of several distinguished citizens nearby, Early dispatched two brigades of cavalry under the commander of Brig. Gen. John McCausland to Chambersburg, Pennsylvania, with orders to demand $500,000 in greenbacks as indemnity for the residences destroyed; if the townspeople refused to pay, McCausland was to burn the city. When the members of the town council stated that they had no intention of complying, McCausland at 9 A.M. on July 30 set the city ablaze. By nightfall half the town had been reduced to ashes.[29]

By this time, the Confederates' continued presence in the Valley had become a considerable annoyance to Grant in his attempts to defeat Lee. Early's march on the Federal capital had forced him to transfer two full army corps from the Petersburg front to quell the fears of the administration, and the subsequent raid against Chambersburg had upset many of the politicians in Washington, the complaints of whom Grant did not want to hear.

Determined to remove Early as a threat to the northern capital and close off the Valley permanently as an avenue of invasion and source of supply, Grant on August 5, 1864, placed Maj. Gen. Philip H. Sheridan in command of all military forces in northern Virginia. The next day he sent his new commander detailed instructions on how he wanted him to conduct the upcoming campaign: "In pushing up the Shenandoah Valley . . . it is desirable that nothing should be left to invite the enemy to return. Take all provisions, forage, and stock wanted for the use of your command. Such as cannot be consumed, destroy." To ensure that there was no misunderstanding in what he expected, Grant repeated his orders to Sheridan three weeks later, telling him to give the enemy no rest and if possible to follow him to the Virginia Central Railroad. "Do all the damage to railroads and crops you can. . . . If the war is to last another year, we want the Shenandoah Valley to remain a barren waste." After two failures, Grant had finally found a general on whom he could rely to successfully carry out his directives. Sheridan was a tough, pugnacious man who loved combat and never backed away from a fight; in following his orders, he would hound Early to his death.[30]

Although reluctant at this time to become embroiled in active combat, Sheridan did not have his troops standing idle. Until the army actually began its advance against the enemy, a considerable number of the men were kept busy going about the countryside burning crops and driving off livestock from farms throughout the Lower Valley.[31] Matthella Harrison described most vividly the destruction inflicted by a squad of Yankee cavalry that descended upon Berryville one August morning:

> Fires of barns, stockyards, etc. soon burst forth and by eleven, from high elevation, fifty could be seen blazing forth. The whole country was enveloped with smoke and fire. The sky was lurid and but for the green trees one might have imagined the shades of Hades had descended suddenly. The shouts, ribald jokes, awful oaths, demoniacal laughter of the fiends added to the horrors of the day. . . . In almost every instance every head of stock was driven off. Those young animals that refused to go were shot down. . . . Large families of children were left without one cow. In many of the barns were stowed . . . wagons, plows, etc., and in no instance did they allow anything to be saved.

Mary Lee wrote in her diary about the numerous outrages committed by the Federals in Winchester. "I did not mention the devastation of the country by the Yankees . . . barns, wheat, crops were all burned; stock and cattle of every kind stolen or destroyed—houses plundered. Mrs. Stother Jones' arms were bruised by the rough grasp of the ruffians who were taking her jewels and money from her."[32]

Finished laying waste to much of the Lower Valley, Sheridan turned his attention to a more important matter—the defeat of Early. Ready to move forward by mid-September, Sheridan attacked the Confederates just outside of Winchester on the nineteenth with his entire force. For the first few hours the graycoats held their own, but in the late afternoon the Federals' greater numbers began to take their toll. Federal cavalry flanked the Rebel left, and the line broke a short time later, many of the men fleeing in panic. With his line disintegrating and the possibility of being enveloped from the left, Early had no alternative but to withdraw, the army retreating to Newtown, 7 miles south of the city. The next morning the Confederates continued to fall back south another 13 miles, until they reached Fisher's Hill, the next defensible position. Confederate losses in the battle were heavy: More than 3,600 men, almost 40 percent of Early's command, were killed, wounded, or missing.

Three days later, Sheridan attacked and defeated the Confederate army again, this time even more decisively. Early lost another 1,000 men, most of them prisoners, and the remainder of the troops did not stop running until they reached Waynesboro, 70 miles south at the base of the Blue Ridge

Mountains. After the defeats of Winchester and Fisher's Hill, one Confederate soldier stated that "the army was so de-moralized that nothing but the perfect security of the mountain fastness in which it had found shelter saved it from going to pieces."[33]

Early, however, had no intention of leaving the Valley to the Federals. After re-forming his command at Waynesboro, where it was reinforced by Lee to its original number, Early planned to strike his opponent at the first opportunity. He did not have to wait long. Following behind as the Federals retired north, the Confederates just before dawn on the morning of October 19 attacked the Union army at Cedar Creek a few miles north of Strasburg and drove the unsuspecting bluecoats from their camp. Confederate success seemed complete, but Early made the fatal mistake of not following up on his attack, and he allowed the dispirited Federals to retreat down the Valley unmolested.

At the time of the attack, Sheridan was not in command of his army. Two weeks earlier, he and several members of his staff had traveled to Washington to confer with the army chief of staff, Henry Hallack, and Secretary of War Edwin M. Stanton about the army's future operations. On the morning of October 19, Sheridan was in Winchester preparing to rejoin the army, when he heard what sounded like muffled gunfire in the distance. It disturbed him. During his ride back, the sound of the battle intensified, and the road soon became jammed with soldiers attempting to flee. Sensing danger, Sheridan broke into a full gallop. As he neared the battlefield, his presence electrified the men, who fell back into the ranks by the thousands. By early afternoon, the Union line had been restored. Sheridan then counterattacked and drove the Confederates from the field, routing them so completely that they never again were an effective fighting force.[34]

From a military standpoint, Sheridan's campaign was a total success. The Confederates had been totally defeated and just about run out of the Valley. Never again during the war would they use the Valley as an avenue to threaten or invade Maryland, Pennsylvania, or Washington, D.C. Sheridan received universal acclaim for laying waste to the rich agricultural resources of the Valley where, between September 26 and October 8, his cavalry put to the torch everything of value, the consequences of which proved disastrous to the Confederacy. Scholars have maintained that the loss of supplies hastened the fall of Richmond, as the Army of Northern Virginia faced increased starvation soon after. It has been said that in consequence of the Valley's being destroyed, Lee's army within weeks was forced to subsist "on a pint of corn meal and an ounce of bacon per day."

But there is a wide array of evidence, much of it in Sheridan's own words, that demonstrates that the destruction of the Valley, though colorful and dramatic, did not deprive the Confederacy of any substantial quantities of subsistence. First and foremost was the fact that the Confederates had long ceased to look upon the Valley—or any other section of Virginia—as a mainstay of supply for the army. From the perspective of the War Department, the resources of the Valley and the rest of the state had been depleted by the end of 1862. By the summer of 1864, this fact had only become more pronounced. On August 22, in response to a dispatch from Lee in which he stated that the army had just consumed the last reserve of corn, Secretary Seddon could only tell the general: "Of corn, I regret to say, there is literally none until the new crop comes in, and the scarcity of it, with the prospects of a bad crop, diminished largely the quantity of wheat which can be spared from the wants of the people." The same was true of oats; only small quantities, not even enough to feed the animals of the army, could be found.

The situation was even more discouraging regarding meat. In May Northrop reported that only 423,000 pounds of bacon and pork and less than 2,200 head of cattle were available in all of Virginia. Things only got worse in the months to come and on September 15 Maj. Seth B. French, of the Subsistence Department, informed Northrop: "[The] collection of meat from *all sources* during the past thirty days would not subsist the Army of Northern Va. for one week. . . . In Virginia the meat supply has been exhausted." Sufficient quantities could not even be found to meet the demands of the civilian population. By October, Georgia, Alabama, and Mississippi were the only states where beef cattle could still be found in any numbers; every army still operating in the field was dependent on those states for its supplies.[35]

On top of that, there was the weather. Like two years earlier, Valley farmers had to contend with a severe drought at the height of the growing season, the consequences of which once again proved devastating. Throughout June, July, and August, farmers could only watch helplessly as their crops withered and died under the hot, blistering sun. "You are no doubt informed of the great drought we are having," Marcus Buck wrote his son in early July. "It is truly distressing. My own loss is especially severe. . . . My last planting of corn has been negated." Three weeks later, he again complained to his son about the drought's adverse impact: "The drought still continues, and it looks as if the effects must be almost fatal to us. I am sure you have never seen such a one and have never seen the country look so gloomy and desolate." Laura Lee wrote in her diary in late July: "We have been suffering for weeks from the most distressing drought. Everything is parched up and the dust perfectly stifling." A crop report in the *Lexington Gazette* in early August summed up the situation: "The wheat crop is of excellent quality, but in quantity will not realize the expectations of the people. . . . Oats are exceedingly short owing to the dry weather. This crop is almost a failure. We have never seen corn look worse at this season. Without rain at a very early date, we will not raise enough to supply bread. Grass is also very short, and much of it was destroyed by our own and the Yankee army in their passage through the Valley. The supply of hay will fall short of home demand."[36]

Further evidence that the Valley's resources had been depleted can be found in a number of Sheridan's dispatches. From the start of the campaign, there were indications that he knew large quantities of subsistence could no longer be obtained from the region. On August 13, 1864, only a week after he assumed command, Sheridan informed Grant that Early had not collected any supplies while he was in the Valley. "There is nothing in the Valley but wheat and a few fine mules. The sum total of all Early's transportation is 250 wagons. He has not sent off or accumulated any supplies. He was simply living off the country." The next day he told Hallack in Washington that supply problems would soon force him to fall back from his present line just south of Winchester to a position farther north. "This line cannot be held," he said, "nor can I supply my command beyond that point with the ten days' rations with which I started. . . . I will destroy all the wheat and hay in the country (there is nothing else), and make it as untenable as possible for the rebel force to subsist."[37]

Even after the battle of Winchester, as the Federal army left the Lower Valley and moved south, correspondence clearly shows that the men were not living off the countryside. On September 21, two days after the battle, Gen. John D. Stevenson, commander at Harpers Ferry and the chief officer charged with keeping the army supplied, notified Sheridan that he would forward all the cattle required for the front the following day, along with additional medical supplies for the wounded. Two days later, 3rd Cavalry Division commander James H. Wilson notified army headquarters from Buckton, west of Front Royal, that his troops were out of provisions, their horses were worn out, and little forage was available. And in a dispatch from his headquarters 6 miles south of New Market the next day, Sheridan told Grant: "I am eighty miles from Martinsburg and find it exceedingly difficult to supply this army. The engagements of Winchester and Fisher's Hill broke up my original plan of pushing up the Valley with a certain amount of supplies and then returning. There is not sufficient in the Valley to live off the country." In response, Grant urged his subordinate to make every effort possible to procure additional subsistence for his command and move east of the Blue Ridge so he could destroy the enemy supply depot at Charlottesville and the adjacent rail lines. But Sheridan balked at the proposal, telling his superior on the twenty-ninth that he could not accumulate sufficient supplies to do so.[38]

In the same dispatch, however, Sheridan informed Grant that the countryside from Harrisonburg to Staunton had abundant forage and grain, and that he intended to deprive the enemy of it by destroying it. "The destruction of the grain and forage . . . ," he said, "will be a terrible blow to them." Continuing to boast about the destruction his forces had inflicted upon the region, Sheridan wrote to Grant two days later: "I have devastated the Valley from Staunton down to Mount Crawford, and will continue. The destruction of mills, grain, forage, foundries, & c., is very great."[39]

The contradictions in Sheridan's statements raise some interesting questions. First, if abundant provisions could still be found in the region, why did Sheridan tell Grant that he was having difficulty keeping his army supplied as it marched up the Valley? Also, if subsistence could still be obtained, why did he tell Grant that supply problems would make it impossible for him to move east of the Blue Ridge and advance on Charlottesville? The distance from Staunton to Charlottesville is no more than 40 miles, so vast stores would not have been needed. By a forced march, Sheridan could have been there in a day and a half. Moreover, he would have had no one to stand in his way; the Confederate army was in complete disarray in the aftermath of their two defeats and would have been unable to contest his advance. But the most intriguing question that needs to be asked is, if vast quantities of supplies could still be found in the Valley, why was the Confederacy going to all the trouble of feeding Lee's army with foodstuffs from the Deep South, more than 600 miles distant? With the railroads deteriorating daily, is seems inconceivable that all those concerned with keeping the troops supplied—Northrop, Lawton, Seddon, Lee, and the local commanders in the Valley—would have overlooked a major source of subsistence so close to the army.

Sheridan has been credited with burning out the Valley and denying the Confederates the use of its resources, and his statements of what he destroyed have been readily accepted as fact and have never truly been challenged. But on closer examination, it is clear that he grossly magnified—and in numerous instances invented—the figures of what his forces captured or destroyed during the campaign.[40] That Sheridan did so is apparent on studying the actions of the Federal cavalry and the reports of their commanders between September 25 and October 8.

The prevailing view of the campaign has been that after the Federal army reached Harrisonburg on September 25, Sheridan dispersed his three divisions of cavalry across the width of the Valley with orders to destroy anything that could support the enemy. There, for the next ten days, his troops systematically laid waste to everything between Harrisonburg and Staunton, burning all crops, barns, gristmills, and lumber mills, and driving off or confiscating all cattle, sheep, pigs, and horses. Then, with the Upper Valley destroyed, Sheridan from October 6 to 8 inflicted the same punishment on the entire region between Harrisonburg and Winchester as the army retired north. But the reports of his officers disclose that Sheridan's three divisions of horsemen actually spent very little of their time savaging the countryside. In fact, between September 26 and October 6, the cavalry spent little more than two days burning crops and driving off livestock between Harrisonburg and Staunton.

On September 26, the 3rd Cavalry Division, along with the Reserve Brigade of the 1st Division, led by the cavalry commander Maj. Gen. Alfred Torbert, advanced on Staunton and destroyed the railroad station and Confederate supply depot. After capturing 25 wagons, 65 head of cattle, 50 horses, 125 barrels of hard bread, 100 barrels of flour, 5 tons of salt, 500 bales of hay, and small amounts of other military stores, Torbert the next day marched on Waynesboro, where, on the twenty-eighth, he sacked the government buildings and destroyed the railroad bridge that spanned the South Fork of the Shenandoah River. Thereafter, Torbert and his command retired to Bridgewater, a few miles south of Harrisonburg, where they remained in camp until the army moved north on October 6.[41]

During this same period, the 1st and 2nd Divisions spent even less time— only one day—carrying out Grant's instructions to make the Valley a "barren waste." On September 29 the 2nd Division, commanded by Brig. Gen. George Custer, marched south from Cross Keys to Mount Sidney and then back north on the Valley Pike to Mount Crawford. In the course of their travels, Custer reported, his troops destroyed 9 large mills, about 100 barns containing wheat and hay, and a large number of stacks of grain and hay in the fields, and brought in about 150 head of cattle and 500 sheep. The accomplishments of the 1st Division were relatively minor as well. Thomas C. Devin, commander of the 2nd Brigade, reported that his troops, while traveling south from Port Republic to Piedmont and then back north to Mount Crawford, destroyed 82 barns containing hay and grain, 72 stacks of hay and grain, 5 flour mills, 2 sawmills, an iron furnace, and 2 wagons loaded with grain and flour, and drove in 321 head of cattle and 20 sheep. In his report, Col. James H. Kidd of the 1st Brigade said only that his troops had destroyed a large amount of property and driven in a large number of cattle and other stock. Considering that only one part of one regiment had been assigned to carry out the orders, it would be reasonable to believe that the quantities were about equal to those of Devin's brigade. Afterward, the two divisions, like Torbert's, remained in camp or on picket duty until the army retired back down the Valley.[42]

Thus far, as evidenced by the reports of Sheridan's commanders, the efforts of the Federals had been less than spectacular. Overall, only a small amount of livestock had been taken or driven off, and except for destroying the railroad station, the bridge over the Shenandoah River, and the supply depots at Staunton and Waynesboro, only the small triangular region between Port Republic, Mount Sidney, and Mount Crawford had felt the wrath of the Federals. The rest of the country between Harrisonburg and Staunton remained untouched. One individual who realized as much was Jedediah Hotchkiss. "The Yankees," he told his brother from Mount Sidney a couple days after they had retired to Harrisonburg, "did but little damage in Augusta county; burned a few barns and mills in the lower end of the county." But in transmitting his army's accomplishments to Grant, Sheridan painted an entirely different picture. "I have devastated the Valley from Staunton down to Mount Crawford, and will continue," he told Grant on the morning of October 1. "The destruction of mills, grain, forage, foundries, & c., is very great. The cavalry report to me that they have collected 3,000 head of cattle and sheep between Staunton and Mount Crawford."[43]

Questions about Sheridan's veracity also arise in regard to his inability to move east of the mountains. It was at this stage of the campaign that Grant wanted his subordinate, after destroying the railroad at Staunton, to cross over the Blue Ridge and advance on Charlottesville. But Sheridan objected, stating on September 29 that he could not accumulate sufficient supplies to do so. He continued to voice his reasons for not doing so two days later, telling Grant that he could not obtain enough supplies to carry him through to the Orange and Alexandria Railroad. However, the correspondence of General Stevenson, the officer most responsible for keeping the army supplied, clearly contradicts Sheridan's claims. On October 1, the very day Sheridan told Grant that a lack of provisions would make it impossible for him to cross over the Blue Ridge, Stevenson at Harpers Ferry informed Secretary of War

Edwin Stanton in Washington that Sheridan's chief commissary officer, Capt. William H. Hosack, had reported to him that the army had a week's rations. Four days later, Stevenson again assured Stanton that the troops were well provided for, telling him that supplies for General Sheridan would last until the ninth.[44]

A similar contradiction can be found in Sheridan's argument that he did not have the necessary means of transportation. Averse to crossing over the mountains, Sheridan stated the reasons for his opposition in a dispatch to Grant from his headquarters at Harrisonburg on October 1: "It is no easy matter to pass [through] these mountain gaps and attack Charlottesville, hauling supplies through difficult passes, fourteen miles in length, and with a line of communication from 135 to 145 miles in length, without the organization of supply trains, ordnance trains, and all the appointments of an army making a permanent advance. At present we are organized for a raid up the Valley, with no trains except the corps trains. All the regimental wagons had to be used as supply wagons to subsist us as far as this place, and can't do it at that." Yet, as the numerous dispatches of Stevenson and others show, between September 20 and October 6 Federal trains of 200 to 1,000 wagons were dispatched almost daily from Harpers Ferry or Winchester for the front, so Sheridan would have had available to him all the transportation he required. Moreover, two days after the battle of Winchester, the War Department had begun to rebuild the Orange and Alexandria Railroad, anticipating the need to supply the army after it crossed over the mountains. By October 2 the line had been repaired up to Rappahannock Station, and it would have taken less than a week to complete the railroad to Charlottesville. In response, Sheridan stated that it would have taken an entire corps to protect it, which very well may have been true. But considering the opportunity it would have presented the Federals—a cavalry raid launched from Charlottesville against Burkville would have cut the flow of supplies on the Virginia & Tennessee and the Richmond & Danville Railroads, which would have forced Lee to abandon Richmond—it seems likely that Grant would have been willing to find the troops required to protect the line.[45]

Even after the army began moving north, it is clear from reports that the damage inflicted by the troops was not as all-encompassing as Sheridan professed. The decision having been made not to cross over the Blue Ridge, Sheridan consequently ordered the 2nd Division, led by Brig. Gen. William H. Powell, to advance down the Page Valley east of the Massanutten Mountains and burn out the country down to Luray. Powell left Harrisonburg on the morning of October 1, and after entering the Valley, he commenced "driving off all stock of every description, destroying all grain, burning mills . . . and all forage," until he reached Luray about 40 miles distant the next evening, where the division remained until October 7. That Powell burned or destroyed a considerable amount of grain and drove off some livestock cannot be disputed, but in reporting the extent of Powell's achievements to those in Washington, Sheridan stated that the division had marched as far as Millwood, more than 30 miles north of their current position, cleaning out the entire Valley from Swift Run Gap to Millwood. Sheridan stated further that the troops "were driving before them 3,000 head of stock," yet Powell makes no mention of it in his report.[46]

Sheridan exaggerated his army's achievements even more in the days and weeks following. With no further reason to remain in the Upper Valley, Sheridan and the rest of his command began falling back down the Valley on the morning of October 6, the cavalry trailing behind with instructions to burn all forage and drive off all stock. By the evening of October 7 the army had marched as far north as Woodstock, where Sheridan sent a detailed report to Grant listing the army's accomplishments. "In moving back to this point," he said, "the whole country from the Blue Ridge to the North Mountain has been made untenable for a rebel army. I have destroyed over 2,000 barns, filled with wheat, hay, and farming implements; over 70 mills, filled with flour and wheat; have driven in front of the army over 4,[000] head of stock, and have killed and issued to the troops not less than 3,000 sheep. This destruction embraces the Luray and Little Fort Valley, as well as the main valley." He then told Grant, "To-morrow I will continue the destruction of wheat, forage, & c., down to Fisher's Hill. When this is completed the Valley, from Winchester up to Staunton, ninety-two miles, will have but little in it for man or beast." Several days after his troops had completed the work of burning out the Valley, Sheridan again wrote to Grant, telling his commander, "I have given you but a faint idea of the cleaning out of the stock, forage, wheat, provisions, & c., in the Valley." Once fighting was over, Sheridan submitted a report to the War Department in November stating that his forces during the course of the campaign had captured or destroyed over 435,000 bushels of wheat, 77,000 bushels of corn, 20,000 bushels of oats, 20,000 tons of hay, 10,900 head of cattle, 12,000 sheep, 15,000 swine, 12,000 pounds of ham and bacon, 3,772 horses, 71 flour mills, and 1,200 barns.[47]

The totals in Sheridan's official report are impressive. After examining the reports of his subordinates, however, one has to question the veracity of his report, as his figures are much larger than those of his subordinate commanders who actually carried out the orders, and it seems that in truth, the Federal cavalry destroyed far less than what he claimed. The reports of Brig. Gen. George A. Custer and Thomas C. Devin substantiate this point. Custer was in command of the 2nd Division on September 29 and the 3rd Division when the army retired back down the Valley (after Wilson had been transferred to the west, Custer had assumed command of the 3rd Division). On November 15 he submitted a combined report to army headquarters in which he stated that during the course of the campaign, the forces under his command had destroyed 150 barns filled with wheat and hay, 10 flour mills, 10,000 bushels of wheat, 2,000 bushels of oats, and 1,500 tons of hay; captured 423 horses and 152 head of cattle; and driven off 400 sheep and 100 head of cattle. Devin submitted a detailed account for September 29 and October 8, the two days his brigade was involved in destruction. He stated that his troopers had captured or destroyed 197 barns, 278 stacks of hay and grain, 23 flour mills, 18,000 bushels of wheat, 611 head of cattle, 339 sheep, and 75 hogs. The only other force left to add to the total of what Sheridan reported captured or destroyed was the 1st Brigade of the 1st Cavalry Division, whose best efforts in three days of activity could hardly have made up the difference.[48]

A combination of factors was responsible for the Federals not being as successful in their efforts as Sheridan maintained. First, and probably foremost, was the fact that contrary to popular belief, only a small number, and not all of the cavalry's 6,000 troopers, actually participated in carrying out the orders to ravage the countryside. Prior to the march north, Torbert on October 5 issued orders to Custer and Brig. Gen. Wesley Merritt, 1st Division Commander, stating that individual units would be assigned for the purpose of collecting livestock and burning forage: "Regiments will be detained for this purpose, and the balance of your command will be kept well in hand."[49]

Another contributing factor was time—or the lack of it—which forced the troops to carry out their orders quickly. In their march, the cavalry traveled 20 to 30 miles a day, which did not allow them much time to ravage the countryside. Merritt admitted as much years later, when he stated that the work was done hurriedly, in numerous instances giving citizens throughout the Valley ample time to secret supplies, which many of them did. Time constraints also prevented the Federals from being as thorough as they would have liked, limiting their actions for the most part to the areas along the main roads, the Valley Pike in particular. A Woodstock citizen testified to that fact, complaining to one Yankee in November that they occupied all of their time and effort ravaging those homesteads adjacent to the pike, while leaving those who lived a distance away unscathed. "You folks don't work the thing right, " he told the private. "You only seem to see the main pike, there are hundreds of folks living over in the bottoms, that you never see, the very richest part of the valley, where there are hundreds of acres of splendid corn untouched, while we that live on the pike are literally stripped of everything."[50]

Another factor—and one that has not received much notice—was that many of the soldiers and officers found the assignment of burning out civilians repulsive and made no effort to hide their disapproval. Recording the feelings of his comrades, the historian of the 1st New York Cavalry Regiment wrote that men who had "never flinched in the hottest fight declared they would have no hand in this burning." Col. James Kidd, of the 6th Michigan Cavalry, described the incendiarism as a most "disagreeable business," and after reading his account of the burning of a mill in Port Republic, one can readily understand why:

> The mill in the little hamlet of Port Republic contained the means of livelihood—the food of the women and children whom the exigencies of war had bereft of their natural providers and, when they found that it was the intention to destroy that on which their very existence seemed to depend, their appeals to be permitted to have some of the flour before the mill was burned, were heartrending. Worse than all else, in spite of the most urgent precautions . . . the flames extended. The mill stood in the midst of a group of wooden houses and some of them took fire. Seeing the danger, I . . . ordered every man to fall in and assist in preventing the further spread of the flames, an effort which was, happily, successful. What I saw there is burned into my memory. Women with children in their arms, stood in the street and gazed frantically upon the threatened ruin of their homes, while the tears rained down their cheeks. The anguish pictured in their faces would have melted any heart not seared by the horrors and "necessities" of war. It was too much for me and at the first moment that duty would permit, I hurried away from the scene. General Merritt did not see these things, nor did General Sheridan, much less General Grant.[51]

But orders were orders, and despite their own feelings, the men for the most part carried them out faithfully, though on a number of occasions they took it upon themselves to grant a few lucky souls a reprieve. Directed one day to torch all the barns in the vicinity of Dayton, a small community south of

Harrisonburg, a detachment of the 2nd Ohio just went through the motions, setting fire to only a few. "Many barns . . . were not burned," wrote Roger Hannaford, one of the troopers. "I saw the boys . . . helping an old lady to move her furniture, as they had rec'd orders to burn the barn & this stood near the house, but as it was near evening, when the officer left them, the boys all left, not one of them would fire the barn."[52]

All this is not to say that Sheridan did not inflict a considerable degree of devastation upon the region. He did. In the wake of the campaign, thousands of families throughout the Valley faced the prospect of abject starvation. "Our county has been devastated and many of our people have been left without the means of supporting life through the coming winter," Marcus Buck said shortly after the Federal onslaught. "Nearly all the slaves, horses, cattle, hogs and sheep have been taken, and in the vicinity of the camps where ever they have been, the houses have been divested of everything valuable." James Schreckhire, of Augusta County, described to his brother how the Federals had destroyed most of his property and crops, as well as those of his neighbors, and said that "there will be suffering times in the valley this winter as the Yanks have burnt all of the barns . . . & all of the mills except one occasionally. . . . Some people are ruined entirely."[53]

The civilian inhabitants were not the only ones facing hard times. In light of the devastation, the remnants of Early's shattered command also found it increasingly more difficult to obtain provisions and forage. In order to get by, many of the men were forced to go out into the countryside and pick corn. "The government is husking all the corn in the fields," one soldier told his wife from their camp near New Market in November. "In fact it is all gone in Rockingham and Shenandoah countys now. Augusta may look out next." Several resourceful members of the Richmond Howitzers of the 1st Virginia Artillery traded their services for food. "Our mess," Pvt. Creed Davis told his wife, "is shucking corn for a farmer who will pay us for our services in flour. In the absence of rations."[54]

As soldiers, those in the army had no choice but to remain, but the same did not apply when it came to the civilian population. With their property and the ability to provide for themselves destroyed, and tired of the war, hundreds more families packed up the few possessions they still had and moved away. Many of those who did so were from certain religious denominations, the Dunkers and Mennonites in particular. From the vicinity of Harrisonburg alone, it was reported that over 400 wagons, loaded with people and belongings, followed the Federal army as it retired down the Valley in October.[55]

The dire state of the war added to the atmosphere of despair. Despite their best efforts and prayers, events continued to go downhill for the Confederacy. Aside from Sheridan's victory in the Valley, Grant had what appeared to be a death grip on Lee and the Army of Northern Virginia outside of Richmond and Petersburg. In September Sherman had captured Atlanta, and in the months following, he proceeded to march his army across Georgia, cutting a swath of destruction 60 miles wide, from Atlanta to the coastal city of Savannah. Worst of all, the Northern victories had assured Lincoln's reelection, which everyone knew meant that the war would continue until the bitter end.

In the Valley, the people could do nothing but watch as their dreams of independence were crushed by the unrelenting power of their opponent. While still hoping that their forces would somehow prevail, many an individual surely must have known that the end was close at hand.[56]

EPILOGUE

The Federal victory at Cedar Creek marked the end of military operations in the Shenandoah Valley for 1864. With the campaign over, the two armies over the course of the next two months were for all practical purposes disbanded, as both Lee and Grant began recalling units back to the front at Richmond. Lee initiated the process by ordering Kershaw's division back to Petersburg on November 15. Two weeks later, Grant directed the 6th Corps and a division of cavalry to return to the Army of the Potomac. The Federal commander soon after had a second division of cavalry transferred to Cumberland, Maryland, for the winter. Lee reacted to his opponent's moves by recalling what remained of the 2nd Corps from the Valley in mid-December. By December Early and what force he had left went into winter quarters at Staunton. The Federals were content for a while to remain in their camp at Cedar Creek; eventually they established winter quarters just outside Winchester.[1]

As farmer James Schreckhire had predicted a short time earlier, the Valley's populace did indeed suffer during the winter of 1864–65. "My heart breaks for the poor among us, too numerous for my little store of supplies," Marcus Buck told his son in late January. "Many persons are almost destitute of food for their families and their stock." Trooper John Hannaford, encamped with his cavalry regiment on a farm outside Winchester, could not help but notice the hardship the farmer was going through or feel sympathetic toward his plight. "He had a good crop of corn & hay," Hannaford said, but "the rebels took considerable of both, our men took the rest, & now he has nothing to feed his cows & horses but little he can beg or buy from soldiers; not a fence rail is left on his farm." In the days following, all the boards from his barn disappeared, and the soldiers even tore down and carried away his privy.

A veteran soldier, Hannaford realized that the people of the North understood little about the war's terrible cruelties and the pain it inflicted on those in its path. "Folks at home know nothing of war," he wrote in his diary. "God grant that they never will. May you all be saved from seeing such scenes of desolation and ruin [as] I have witnessed the last 10 months. . . . I cannot but help pitying the suffering Southern women, and still more the little children."[2]

One such woman was Cornelia McDonald, who, since her husband's death in December, had to care for her seven children by herself. What little money she had had was gone, and it was only through the assistance of friends that she was able to make ends meet. Even then, the children received only two meals a day consisting of beans and molasses, and Mrs. McDonald generally had little more than coffee and a roll. "We had barely enough food to keep from actual want," she wrote later. When she went into town one day with $100 to get supplies, all she returned home with was a "pound of fat bacon, three candles, eighteen dollars for the three, and a pound of bad butter."[3]

Anxious to provide for their families, just about everyone currently facing the prospect of military service applied for an exemption. As happened the previous spring, James Davidson and John Harris soon found themselves flooded with requests from individuals to intercede on their behalf. In light of the fact that the Federals had destroyed many of their farming implements, farmers around the Valley also asked that those craftsmen necessary to their efforts in working their land also be released from the draft. Speaking on behalf of Moses Mason, a wagon- and toolmaker residing in Rockingham County, more than a dozen farmers sent a joint petition to the secretary of war requesting that he be allowed to remain at home "in order that he may be able to supply the wants of a very large section of the farming interests of this county."[4]

But in all fairness, not all of the Valley's men attempted to avoid their military obligation. Three weeks short of his seventeenth birthday, Harry McDonald in late March had finally persuaded his mother to let him join the army. However, the young man reached the field only in time to take part in the army's retreat from Richmond, and to his mother's great relief, he returned home a short time later. But Harry covered his face with his hands and wept as he entered the house, muttering to himself, "To think it is all over and I did not strike a blow."[5]

Since the start of the year, the fortunes of the Confederacy had continued their downward spiral. In mid-January a Federal force stormed and captured Fort Fisher at Wilmington, North Carolina, the last remaining Rebel port and link to the outside world. Sherman advanced into South Carolina the following month and before long had taken possession of Fort Sumter and Columbia, the state capital, about half of which was burnt to the ground. Toward the end of March, Sherman, now having made his way into North Carolina, again defeated the Confederates, this time at Bentonville, 50 miles southeast of Raleigh.

During this same period, the Valley also was the scene of hostilities for one last time. On February 20, 1865, Grant ordered Sheridan to destroy the Confederate supply base at Lynchburg, as well as the James Canal and the adjacent railroad lines in all directions, making sure they would be of no possible use to the enemy during the upcoming campaign. Sheridan marched south a week later, his 10,000 cavalrymen reaching Staunton on March 1. The next day the Federal column headed east toward Charlottesville. Shortly after midday they confronted Early's small command, no more than 2,000 men, at Waynesboro at the base of the Blue Ridge Mountains. There the Federals in short order routed the Confederates from their position, scattering them in all directions. Early and his staff managed to escape, but they were about the only to do so; over 1,500 troops and all of the artillery were captured during the engagement.[6]

Declining in proportion to the Confederates' sagging military fortunes was the morale of the Valley's inhabitants. "In every piece of intelligence from our lines before Richmond," wrote Cornelia McDonald at the start of February, "there was now matter for discouragement and apprehension. It was plain that things were not going favourably." She was even more pessimistic the following month: "March came in gloomy and melancholy, and brought with it a dreadful certainty of disaster and defeat. One thing that almost quenched the last hope in me, was seeing the men coming home; every day they passed, in squads, in couples, or singly, all leaving the army." Still grieving over the death of his son Robert, killed outside Richmond in June, and concerned about his other son, Francis, now imprisoned in Fort Delaware, Francis McFarland held out little hope that the representatives sent to the Peace Conference in Washington at the start of February would return successful in their mission.[7]

Expecting defeat, the people did not have to wait long before their fears were realized. In an attempt to break the Union stranglehold on Richmond and Petersburg, Lee on March 25, in what would be the army's last offensive, attacked Fort Stedman, a redoubt guarding part of the Federal line opposite Petersburg. Though the Confederates were successful at first, capturing the fort and sections of trench on both sides, the Yankees after a couple of hours reformed their lines and forced the Rebels to abandon the fort and return to their former position. On April 2 the Confederates were forced to evacuate Richmond, and a week later, on April 9, 1865, Lee and the Army of Northern

Virginia were finally brought to heel at Appomattox, a small, quiet village some 70 miles west of Richmond. Three days later, the Confederate army formally surrendered, and the war in Virginia was over—and in reality, it was over in the rest of the country as well.

Although they had been aware that Lee could not hold out much longer, the announcement of his surrender nevertheless shocked many a Valley resident. Lexington resident Margaret Preston had a hard time accepting the fact. "News has come that Lee's army has surrendered!" she exclaimed. "We are dumb with astonishment! Why then all these four years of suffering—of separations—of horror—of blood—of havoc—of awful bereavement! Why these ruined homes—these broken family circles—these scenes of terror that must scathe the brain of those who witnessed them till their deaths." Rev. William S. White, realizing the hatred felt toward the South by the Northerners, foresaw the wave of retribution that would be imposed by a vengeful foe, now victorious. "Our capital and commonwealth are now under the heel of our enemy. Scarcely a doubt exists that we are to be a subjected people, ruined as to all political power, and sorely straitened for a time for the necessities of life."[8]

The reverend was correct in his assessment. The South would in many respects become a vanquished land. And for many at first it would be a struggle to survive. But the residents of the Shenandoah Valley, though angered and bitterly disappointed, did not let the defeat consume them. Rather than hold on to the past, they chose instead to look to the future, rebuilding their homes and farms and lives, before long restoring the Valley to its former beauty.

Appendix A

Production of Major Grains and Livestock for the Counties of the Shenandoah Valley in 1860

MAJOR GRAINS
(Bushels, Tons)

	Wheat	Corn	Oats	Rye	Hay (tons)
Augusta	307,402	752,530	191,379	57,479	21,087
Berkeley	237,576	275,525	76,176	18,672	8,031
Clarke	330,153	252,205	53,205	14,041	3,126
Frederick	224,471	285,770	85,241	27,677	7,777
Jefferson	422,514	358,267	54,798	15,198	6,259
Page	102,149	175,168	21,384	27,438	4,104
Rockbridge	193,338	423,952	138,298	18,889	9,638
Rockingham	358,653	684,239	128,010	45,362	19,174
Shenandoah	172,292	195,778	45,289	10,635	6,455
Warren	104,776	175,168	28,181	24,629	2,561
Valley Totals	2,453,324	3,562,529	821,961	260,020	88,212
State Totals	13,130,977	38,319,999	10,186,720	944,330	445,133
Valley as % of State	18.6%	9.3%	8.1%	27.5%	19.8%

LIVESTOCK

	Horses	Swine	Sheep	Beef cattle	Milk cows
Augusta	8,852	31,033	13,013	14,206	6,441
Berkeley	3,510	13,469	7,057	3,687	2,768
Clarke	2,631	9,642	6,971	3,195	1,568
Frederick	4,084	12,939	9,892	5,420	2,926
Jefferson	3,421	15,044	7,296	4,071	2,316
Page	2,169	10,083	3,472	3,176	1,700
Rockbridge	4,381	18,762	10,298	9,227	4,046
Rockingham	7,874	37,307	13,364	13,299	6,011
Shenandoah	2,677	8,905	3,742	4,340	2,071
Warren	1,405	7,240	5,299	4,406	1,365
Valley Totals	41,037	164,424	80,307	65,027	31,208
State Totals	287,679	1,599,919	1,043,269	615,882	330,713
Valley as % of State	**14.3%**	**10.3%**	**7.7%**	**10.6%**	**9.4%**

APPENDIX B

Federal Reports of
Property Captured or Destroyed
During the Valley Campaign of 1864

OFFICIAL REPORT OF PHILIP H. SHERIDAN

Horses	3,772	Hay (tons)	20,397
Flour mills	71	Fodder (tons)	500
Barns	1,200	Straw (tons)	450
Wheat (bushels)	435,802	Beef cattle	10,918
Corn (bushels)	77,176	Sheep	12,000
Oats (bushels)	20,000	Swine	15,000
Flour (bushels)	874	Calves	250
Bacon and hams (pounds)	12,000	Mules	545

Property Captured

	1st Division	2nd Division	3rd Division	Totals
Horses	134	2,000	423	2,557
Beef cattle	—	7,000	152	7,152

Property Destroyed

	1st Division	2nd Division	3rd Division	Totals
Barns	630	—	150	780
Flour mills	47	—	10	57
Wheat (bushels)	410,742	—	10,000	420,742
Oats (bushels)	750	—	2,000	2,750
Flour (barrels)	560	—	—	560
Corn (acres)	515	—	—	515
Fodder (tons)	272	—	—	272
Hay (tons)	3,455	—	1,500	4,955
Straw (tons)	255	—	—	255
Cattle driven off	1,347	—	100	1,447
Sheep driven off	1,231	—	400	1,631
Swine driven off	725	—	—	725

As the tables illustrate, the two commanders' reports differ considerably. This study, however, does not contend that one is accurate and the other is not. It maintains that both are highly inaccurate and cannot be considered valid. In addition, the report of the cavalry, submitted by Gen. Alfred Torbert, seems contrived. When Sheridan burned out the Valley, he stated that he deployed his three divisions of cavalry across the entire corridor, with orders to drive off all stock and destroy all supplies as they moved northward. Under those circumstances, the three divisions should have shared fairly equally in the destruction of crops and the confiscation of livestock. But Torbert's report reveals a completely different pattern. The 1st Division has been credited with destroying all the wheat and other grains but capturing no livestock, while it appears that the 2nd did the exact opposite, doing nothing but seizing cattle and horses. Also, if close to 40,000 head of livestock were seized, as Sheridan stated in his report, what did he do with them? In the Official Records, there is only a single dispatch that even mentions the collection of livestock, and then only in passing.

But even if one were to accept Sheridan's statements of what he captured and destroyed as being completely accurate, the totals only serve to demonstrate how far the agricultural productivity of the Valley had declined. If the figures in his report are compared to the statistics of the 1860 census for the five counties—Augusta, Rockingham, Shenandoah, Page, and Warren—primarily devastated by the Federal cavalry in the campaign, they show a decline of 60 percent in wheat, 64 percent in hay, and 70 to 84 percent in horses, cattle, sheep, and hogs. Moreover, the total amounts of corn, oats, flour, bacon and hams, fodder, and straw destroyed are insignificant even in Sheridan's report. One also has to question how Sheridan compiled the totals for his report, as his numbers except in wheat do not come anywhere close to Torbert's.

Credited with burning out the Valley and denying the Confederates of its resources, Sheridan in actuality did little more than destroy what remained for local consumption. The primary reason the Army of Northern Virginia teetered on the verge of starvation during the latter stages of the war was not Sheridan's destruction of the Valley, but rather the total inefficiency and collapse of the Confederacy's railroads.

NOTES

CHAPTER 1: "THE DAUGHTER OF THE STARS"

1. Joseph A. Waddell, *Annals of Augusta County, Virginia from 1726–1871* (reprint, Harrisonburg, Va.: C. J. Carrier Company, 1979), 18; John W. Wayland, *The German Element of the Shenandoah Valley of Virginia* (reprint, Bridgewater, Va.: C. J. Carrier Company, 1964), 1–5; Bruce Catton, *A Stillness at Appomattox* (Garden City, N.Y.: Doubleday, 1953), 273; Jeffrey D. Wert, *From Winchester to Cedar Creek: The Shenandoah Valley Campaign of 1864* (Carlisle, Pa.: South Mountain Press, 1976), 26.

2. J. Lewis Peyton, *History of Augusta County* (reprint, Bridgewater, Va.: C. J. Carrier Company, 1953), 5–6; Samuel Kercheval, *A History of the Valley of Virginia*, 3rd ed. (Woodstock, Va.: Grabill, 1902), 37–40.

3. Peyton, *History of Augusta County*, 24–25; Waddell, *Annals of Augusta County*, 18–19; Richard L. Morton, *Colonial Virginia. Volume Two: Westward Expansion and the Prelude to Revolution, 1710–1763* (Chapel Hill: University of North Carolina Press, 1960), 446–48.

4. Howard McKnight Wilson, *Great Valley Patriots* (Verona, Va.: McClure Press, 1976), 4; Wayland, *German Element of the Shenandoah Valley*, 20; Leyburn, *The Scotch-Irish*, 203–7.

5. Thomas D. Gold, *History of Clarke County* (Berryville, Va.: R. C. Hughes, 1914), 13; Wayland, *German Element of the Shenandoah Valley*, 24–26, 32; Wilson, *Great Valley Patriots*, 4; Peyton, *History of Augusta County*, 10.

6. Freeman H. Hart, *The Valley of Virginia in the American Revolution, 1763–1789* (Chapel Hill: University of North Carolina Press, 1942), 114–15, 119, 149, 168–69; John W. Wayland, *A History of Shenandoah County, Virginia* (Strasburg, Va.: Shenandoah Publishing, 1927), 125, 131, 137; Gold, *History of Clarke County*, 30–31.

7. U.S. Government, *The Eighth Census of the United States, 1860: Volume on Manufactures* (Washington, D.C.: Government Printing Office, 1864), 605–34.

8. Ibid., *Volume on Agriculture*, 516–20. This pattern of settlement did not occur in any other section of the state.

9. Frederick Morton, *The Story of Winchester in Virginia* (Strasburg, Va.: Shenandoah Publishing, 1925), 109–11, 123–24, 236–38; Wayland, *A History of Shenandoah County*, 133; Waddell, *Annals of Augusta County*, 436.

10. Robert G. Tanner, *Stonewall in the Valley: Thomas J. "Stonewall" Jackson's Shenandoah Valley Campaign, Spring 1862* (Garden City, N.Y.: Doubleday, 1976), 20.

11. T. K. Cartmell, *Shenandoah Valley Pioneers and Their Descendants* (reprint, Berryville, Va.: Chesapeake Book Company, 1963), 54, 56; Wayland, *A History of Shenandoah County*, 292; Morton, *The Story of Winchester in Virginia*, 100–104.

12. Festus P. Summers, *The Baltimore and Ohio in the Civil War* (New York: G. P. Putnam's Sons, 1939), 44; Cartmell, *Shenandoah Valley Pioneers and Their Descendants*, 59–61.

13. T. K. Cartmell, *Shenandoah Valley Pioneers and Their Descendants*, 62–63; Wayland, *A History of Shenandoah County*, 293.

14. Charles W. Turner, "The Virginia Central Railroad at War, 1861–1865," *The Journal of Southern History* 20 (1942), 511; Douglas Southall Freeman, *Lee's Lieutenants: A Study in Command.* 3 vols. (New York: Charles Scribner's Sons, 1942–44), Vol. 3. endmap.

15. John T. Schlebecker, "Farmers in the Lower Shenandoah Valley, 1850," *The Virginia Magazine of History and Biography*, 79 (1971), 465, 468–71; U.S. Government, *The Seventh Census of the United States, 1850* (Washington, D.C.: Government Printing Office, 1854), 275–80; Jean Gottmann, *Virginia at Mid-Century* (New York: Henry Holt and Company, 1955), 103–4.

16. Schlebecker, "Farmers in the Lower Shenandoah Valley, 1850," 464, 468–69; Waddell, *Annals of Augusta County*, 436; U.S. Government, *The Seventh Census of the United States*, 273–76; Tanner, *Stonewall in the Valley*, 20.

17. U.S. Government, *The Seventh Census of the United States*, 256–57; U.S. Government, *The Eighth Census of the United States*, 154–63; Wayland, *The German Element of the Shenandoah Valley*, 181–83.

18. U.S. Government, *The Eighth Census of the United States*, 154–63; Henry T. Shanks, *The Secession Movement in Virginia, 1847–1861* (Richmond: Garrett and Massie, 1934), 123.

CHAPTER 2: "THE MOST PAINFUL VOTE I EVER GAVE"

1. *Staunton Spectator,* January 17, 1860; Shanks, *The Secession Movement in Virginia,* 104.
2. James M. McPherson, *Battle Cry of Freedom* (New York: Oxford University Press, 1988), 217–19.
3. C. C. Strayer to John T. Harris, May 2, 10, 1860, John T. Harris Papers, Special Collections, Carrier Library, James Madison University, Harrisonburg, Virginia. Placed on deposit by the Harrisonburg-Rockingham Historical Society.
4. R. Summers et al. to Waitman T. Willey, August 29, 1860, Waitman T. Willey Papers, West Virginia and Regional History Collection, WVU Libraries; V. M. Brown to Alexander R. Boteler, August 7 and 10, 1860, Alexander R. Boteler Papers, Special Collections, Duke University Library, Durham, North Carolina; *Charlestown Virginia Free Press,* September 27, October 25, 1860; *Lexington Gazette,* September 9, 13, 27, 1860; *Staunton Spectator,* August 14, October 16, 23, 30, 1860.
5. *Lexington Gazette,* September 13, 1860; *Staunton Spectator,* August 28, 1860; *Charlestown Virginia Free Press,* July 19, 1860.
6. *Staunton Spectator,* November 13, 20, 27, December 18, 1860; Shanks, *The Secession Movement in Virginia,* 123; James D. Davidson to John Letcher, November 18, 1860, James D. Davidson Papers, Wisconsin State Historical Society, Madison, Wisconsin (cited hereafter as Davidson Papers, WSHS); George Junkin to Francis McFarland, January 19, 1861, The Francis McFarland Collection, Special Collections, Alderman Library, University of Virginia, Charlottesville, Virginia.
7. *Rockingham Register and Advertizer,* November 16, 1860; *Harrisonburg Valley Democrat,* reprinted in the *Staunton Spectator,* November 20, 1860; *Lexington Gazette,* November 29, 1860; John D. Imboden to John H. McCue, December 3, 1860, McCue Family Papers, Special Collections, Alderman Library, University of Virginia, Charlottesville, Virginia.
8. Shanks, *The Secession Movement in Virginia,* 134; Letcher quoted in Bruce Catton, *The Coming Fury* (Garden City, N.Y.: Doubleday, 1961), 196; Ralph A. Wooster, *The Secession Conventions of the South* (Princeton, N.J.: Princeton University Press, 1962), 140–41.
9. *Staunton Spectator,* January 8, 15, 22, 1861; *Lexington Gazette,* January 3 and 31, 1861; *Charlestown Virginia Free Press,* January 31, 1861; John T. Harris to Ben, January 15, 1861, Harris Papers, placed on deposit by the Harrisonburg-Rockingham County Historical Society; James D. Davidson to

John Letcher, January 31, 1861, James D. Davidson Papers, University Library, Washington and Lee University, Lexington, Virginia (cited hereafter as Davidson Papers, WLU).

10. James D. Davidson to James B. Dorman, February 13, 1861, James B. Dorman Papers, Rockbridge Historical Society, University Library, Washington and Lee University, Lexington, Virginia; John D. Imboden to John H. McCue, February 12, 1861, McCue Family Papers.

11. John H. Miller to John T. Harris, January 19, 1861; Joseph Lowenback to John T. Harris, January 19, 1861; Moses Walton to John T. Harris, January 29, 1861; James G. France to John T. Harris, January 30, 1861, Harris Papers, placed on deposit by the Harrisonburg-Rockingham Historical Society.

12. *Winchester Republican* quoted in Shanks, *The Secession Movement in Virginia*, 122; James J. White to Colonel Reid, March 18, 1861, *Old Zeus, Life and Letters (1860–1862) of James J. White*, edited by Charles W. Turner (Verona, Va.: McClure Press, 1983), 37.

13. Edward S. Kemper to John T. Harris, December 31, 1860; C. M. Brown to John T. Harris, January 22, 1861, Harris Papers, placed on deposit by the Harrisonburg-Rockingham Historical Society; Edward H. Phillips, "The Lower Shenandoah Valley during the Civil War: The Impact of War upon the Civilian Population and upon Civil Institutions" (Ph.D. Diss., University of North Carolina, Chapel Hill, 1958), 8; entry of January 9, 1861, in the Journal of Rev. B. F. Brooke, Winchester-Frederick County Historical Society Archives, Winchester Virginia.

14. Shelby Foote, *The Civil War: A Narrative* (New York: Random House, 1958), vol. 1, 38; Roy P. Basler, ed., *The Collected Works of Abraham Lincoln* (New Brunswick, N.J.: Rutgers University Press, 1953), vol. 4, 262–71.

15. James D. Davidson to James B. Dorman, March 6, 1861, Davidson Papers, WLU.

16. David F. Riggs, "Robert Young Conrad and the Ordeal of Secession," *The Virginia Magazine of History and Biography*, 86 (1978), 61; *Staunton Vindicator*, March 8, 1861, quoted in Shanks, *The Secession Movement in Virginia*, 176.

17. Phillips, Ph.D. diss., 11; Shanks, *The Secession Movement in Virginia*, 187–88.

18. John T. Harris to John B. Baldwin, March 16, 1861, Harris Papers, placed on deposit by the Harrisonburg-Rockingham Historical Society; Robert Y. Conrad to his wife, March 26, 1861, Robert Y. Conrad Papers, The Virginia Historical Society, Richmond, Virginia; James B. Dorman to James D. Davidson, April 9, 1861, Dorman Papers.

19. Wooster, *Secession Conventions of the South*, 148–49; *Richmond Examiner*, June 6, 1861; James D. Davidson to James B. Dorman, April 16, 1861, Davidson Papers, WLU.

20. James D. Davidson to R. M. T. Hunter, May 2, 1861, Davidson Papers, WLU; James Marshall to Waitman T. Willey, May 11, 1861, Willey Papers; Alexander H. H. Stuart to Waitman T. Willey, May 15, 1861, Willey Papers; Wooster, *Secession Conventions of the South*, 149; Phillips, Ph.D. diss., 102; *Staunton Spectator*, May 28, 1861; *Richmond Examiner*, May 27, 28, 29, 1861; McFarland Diary, May 23, 1861.

CHAPTER 3: "THIS IS ONLY THE BEGINNING, I FEAR"

1. Douglas Southall Freeman, *R. E. Lee: A Biography* (New York: Charles Scribner's Sons, 1934), vol. 1, 473; U.S. War Department, *War of the Rebellion: Official Records of the Union and Confederate Armies* (Washington, D.C.: Government Printing Office, 1880–1901), series I, vol. 2, 784, 802 (hereafter cited as *O.R.*; unless indicated, all references are to series I).

2. John D. Imboden, "Jackson at Harper's Ferry in 1861," in *Battles and Leaders of the Civil War*, edited by Robert U. Johnson and Clarence C. Buel (reprint, New York: Thomas Yoseloff, 1956), vol. 1, 118; Freeman, *R. E. Lee*, vol. 1, 507; *Staunton Spectator*, April 23, May 28, 1861; *Lexington Gazette*, April 25, May 30, 1861; Edward A. Moore, *The Story of a Cannoneer under Stonewall Jackson* (reprint, Alexandria, Va.: Time-Life Books, 1983), 24.

3. Robert Hooke to his family, April 20, 1861, Hooke Papers, Special Collections, Duke University Library, Durham, North Carolina; Reuben to Mollie, April 26, 1861, Margaret B. Burress Collection, Carrier Library, James Madison University, Harrisonburg, Virginia; Thomas Ashby, *The Valley Campaigns* (New York: Neale Publishing, 1914), 26; Moore, *The Story of a Cannoneer*, 22; Strother quoted in Phillips, Ph.D. diss., 47–48.

4. Moore, *The Story of a Cannoneer*, 24; Robert Conrad to Holmes Conrad, April 17, 1861, Robert Y. Conrad Papers, The Virginia Historical Society, Richmond, Virginia.

5. William Hooke to his son, July 11, 1861, Hooke Papers.

6. Margaret L. Cooke to Rose McDonald, May 1, 1861, Marshall McDonald Papers, Special Collections, Duke University Library, Durham, North Carolina; entry of June 9, 1861, in the diary of Harriet H. Griffith, from the Harriet Hollingsworth Griffith Collection, Winchester-Frederick County Historical Archives, Winchester, Virginia; Cornelia McDonald, *A*

Diary with Reminiscences of the War and Refugee Life in the Shenandoah Valley, 1860–1865 (Nashville: Cullom & Ghertner, 1934), 19; Brooke Journal, June 24, 1861; *O.R.* 51, pt. 2, 49, 58–59.

7. Ibid., 814, 901, 924.

8. Ibid., 880–81, 889, 897, 907–8, 929–30.

9. Entry for July 4, 1861, in The War Time Diary of Julia Chase, 1861–1864, Handley Regional Library, Winchester, Virginia.

10. *Staunton Spectator*, April 23, 1861; *Winchester Republican*, September 27, 1861; *Lexington Gazette*, April 25, 1861.

11. McFarland Diary, May 19, 1861; Griffith Diary, June 6, 1861; *Winchester Republican*, August 20, 1861; *Lexington Gazette*, August 23, 1861.

12. Chase Diary, July 2, 4, 7, 8, 1861; Brooke Journal, June 16, 22, 29, July 12 and 20, 1861; Mollie to Reuben, July 12, 1861, Burress Collection; Mary White to her father, October 19, 1861, Mary Louisa Reid-White Papers, Rockbridge Historical Society, The University Library, Washington and Lee University, Lexington, Virginia; *Lexington Gazette*, August 23, October 24, 1861.

13. Griffith Diary, June 16, 1861.

14. Phillips, Ph.D. diss., 326–27.

15. U.S. Government, *The Eighth Census of the United States, Volume on Manufactures*, 604–39; *O.R.* 51, pt. 2, 587–88; Griffith Diary, 15; Phillips, Ph.D. diss., 327.

16. Phillips, Ph.D. diss., 327–28.

17. James Reilly to William N. Pendleton, July 1, 1861, Pendleton Papers, Southern Historical Collection, Wilson Library, University of North Carolina at Chapel Hill, North Carolina; Griffith Diary, June 9, 1861; Brooke Journal, July 29, 1861.

18. William Hooke to Robert Hooke, July 4, 1861, Hooke Papers; Entries for June 20 and July 4, 1861, in the Diary of Levi Pitman, Levi Pitman Papers, Special Collections, Alderman Library, University of Virginia, Charlottesville, Virginia; *O.R.* 51, pt. 2, 180; Chase Diary, July 6, September 16, 1861; Mollie to Reuben, July 28, 1861, Burress Collection.

19. Mollie to Reuben, June 21 and 24, 1861, Burress Collection; Entry for June 19, 1861, in the Diary of Sarah Morgan McKown, Sarah Morgan McKown Papers, West Virginia and Regional Historical Collections, WVU Libraries; William Hooke to Robert Hooke, July 4, 1861, Hooke Papers; Mr. McGuffin to John B. McGuffin, July 19, 1861, McGuffin Family Papers, Special Collections, Alderman Library, University of Virginia, Charlottesville, Virginia.

20. *O.R.* 5, 817–18.

21. Ibid., 820–21; ibid. 51, pt. 2, 262–63.

22. Mollie to Reuben, July 12, 1861, Burress Collection; *Lexington Gazette*, September 19, 1861; entry for August 7, 1861, in the Treadwell Smith Diary, The Handley Library, Winchester, Virginia; McKown Diary, June 21, August 19, 1861; Griffith Diary, 32.

23. Phillips, Ph.D. diss., 119–20; Joseph Barry, *The Annals of Harpers Ferry* (Martinsburg, W.Va.: Printed at the office of the *Berkeley Union*, 1872), 69; Charles W. Andrews to his wife, May 24 and June 11, 1861, Charles Wesley Andrews Papers, Special Collections, Duke University Library, Durham, North Carolina; McKown Diary, July 7, 1861; C. W. Andrews to Mrs. Bedinger, June 4, 1861, Bedinger-Dandridge Family Papers, Special Collections, Duke University Library, Durham, North Carolina; Chase Diary, July 12 and 15, 1861.

24. Charles W. Andrews to his wife, May 17, 21, 24, June 1 and 11, 1861; Charles W. Andrews to his son, May 24, 1861, Andrews Papers.

25. McKown Diary, June 29, 1861; McFarland Diary, July 2, 3, 4, 5, 8, 9, 1861; William Hooke to Robert Hooke, July 11, 1861, Hooke Papers.

26. Tippie to Lizzie, July 23, 1861, Boteler Papers; McFarland Diary, July 24, 1861; Virginia Bedinger to her mother, July 27, 1861, Bedinger-Dandridge Family Papers.

27. Marcus to Richard, July 26, 1861, Richard Bayly Buck Collection, Special Collections, Alderman Library, University of Virginia, Charlottesville, Virginia; Virginia Bedinger to her mother, July 27, 1861, Bedinger-Dandridge Family Papers; Bruce S. Greenwalt, ed., "Life behind Confederate Lines in Virginia: The Correspondence of James D. Davidson," *Civil War History*, XVI (1970), 226; McDonald Diary, 29; McKown Diary, July 26, 1861; Chase Diary, July 23, 1861; Griffith Diary, 26.

28. McDonald Diary, 29; Virginia Bedinger to her mother, July 27, 1861, Bedinger-Dandridge Family Papers; Tippie to Lizzie, July 23, 1861, Boteler Papers.

29. Chase Diary, July 22 and 27, 1861.

30. Phillips, Ph.D. diss., 93–94, 100; Charles Andrews to his wife, May 17, 1861, Andrews Papers; Edward Pendleton to Waitman T. Willey, May 3, 1861, Willey Papers; *O.R.* 2, 863; *O.R.* 51, pt. 2, 143; James K. Edmondson to his wife, May 25, 1861, James Kerr Edmondson Correspondence, 1856–1896, Rockbridge Historical Society, The University Library, Washington and Lee University, Lexington, Virginia; Alexander Barclay to

Hannah, December 23, 1861, Alexander T. Barclay Papers, The University Library, Washington and Lee University, Lexington, Virginia.

31. Phillips, Ph.D. diss., 96–99.

32. James K. Edmondson to his wife, May 25, 1861, Edmondson Correspondence; Phillips, Ph.D. diss., 108–10.

33. O.R. 2, 881, 897, 940, 948; Phillips, Ph.D. diss., 110; C. G. Chamberlayne, editor, Ham Chamberlayne—Virginian, Letters and Papers of an Artillery Officer in the War for Southern Independence, 1861–1865 (Richmond, Va.: Press of the Dietz Printing Co., Publishers, 1932), 118.

34. Griffith Diary, 14; Chase Diary, August 23, 1861.

35. Chase Diary, August 25, 1861; O.R. 5, 858.

36. Phillips, Ph.D. diss., 103–4; Charles Andrews to his wife, May 23 and 24, June 11, 1861; Andrews Papers; Pitman Diary, June 1, 16, 17, 1861.

37. Public letter of William Sperow, August 13, 1861; William Sperow to the editors of the Berkeley Union, undated; entries for May 28 and 31, June 3, July 8, 21, 29, 1861, in the daybook of William Sperow, William Sperow Papers, Special Collections, Duke University Library, Durham, North Carolina.

38. O.R. series II, vol. 2, 1430–31, 1467, 1530–45; Chase Diary, August 3, 13, 25, 29, September 18, October 11, 1861; McKown Diary, August 22, 1861; O.R. 5, 827–28.

39. O.R. 51, pt. 2, 143; ibid. 5, 919.

40. Chase Diary, August 13, 1861; Tippie to Lettie, August 1861, Boteler Papers.

41. Strother quoted in Phillips, Ph.D. diss., 149–50.

42. O.R. 2, 814–15, 822, 824–25, 948–49.

43. Ibid., 934, 940.

44. Introduction to the Wells J. Hawks Papers, part of the Thomas J. Jackson Collection, Special Collections, Duke University, Durham, North Carolina; O.R. 2, 949, 967.

45. O.R. 5, 833, 835–36.

46. Ibid., 967; Wells J. Hawks to Francis G. Ruffin, December 9, 1861, Hawks Papers; Richard Goff, Confederate Supply (Durham, N.C.: Duke University Press, 1969), 55.

47. O.R. 5, 889–90, 898–99, 919–20; ibid. 51, pt. 2, 363–64.

48. Ibid., 5, 925, 936–38, 942–43, 949, 965; Chase Diary, November 9 and 18, 1861.

49. Mary White to her father, October 19, 1861, Reid–White Papers; Chase Diary, August 15 and 22, September 10 and 22, November 17 and 28, December 3 and 14, 1861.

50. Brooke Journal, October 24, 1861; Araminta Trout to her daughter, November 24, 1861, Jackson-Trout Papers, Special Collections, Duke University Library, Durham, North Carolina; M. C. Trevey to Dear Sir, November 29, 1861, Davidson Papers, WLU.

51. *O.R.* 5, 1011.

52. Ibid., 51, pt 2, 328; ibid. series II, vol. 2, 1530–45; Phillips, Ph.D. diss., 105–6, 125.

53. Mrs. Phillip Williams to William N. Pendleton, August 25, 1861, Pendleton Papers; Reuben Scott to his wife, October 9, 1861, Burress Collection; Jane Buck to Richard Buck, November 2, 1861, Richard B. Buck Collection.

54. Chase Diary, December 15, 1861.

CHAPTER 4: "FRIENDS ARE NO BETTER THAN FOES"

1. McFarland Diary, January 1, 1862; Chase Diary, January 1, 1862; Lucy Rebecca Buck, *Sad Earth, Sweet Heaven: The Diary of Lucy Rebecca Buck, During the War Between the States, Front Royal, Virginia, December 25, 1861–April 15, 1865,* edited by William P. Buck (Birmingham: Cornerstone, 1973), January 1, 1862.

2. McFarland Diary, 88; Chase Diary, February 1, 1862.

3. McFarland Diary, December 31, 1861, January 25 and February 14, 1862; Buck Diary, February 4 and 5, 1862.

4. Mary Scott to Dear Reuben, February 26, 1862, Burress Collection; James D. Davidson to Dear Sir, February 12, 1862, James D. Davidson Papers, Special Collections, Duke University Library, Durham, North Carolina; Mary White to My Dear Father, February 24, 1862, Reid-White Papers; James J. White to Dear Colonel, February 11, 1862, *Letters of James J. White.*

5. Frank Paxton to his wife, February 28, 1862, *The Civil War Letters of General Frank "Bull" Paxton, C.S.A., a Lieutenant of Lee & Jackson,* edited by John Gallatin Paxton (Hillsboro, Tex.: Hill Junior College Press, 1978), 40; R.B.B. to Ma, February 16, 1862, Richard Bayly Buck Transcripts, Special Collections, Alderman Library, University of Virginia, Charlottesville, Virginia.

6. *Winchester Republican*, January 31, 1862; *Staunton Spectator*, February 18, 1862.

7. *O.R.* 5, 965.

8. Tanner, *Stonewall in the Valley*, 69, 75, 78; Ludwell Lee Montague, "Subsistence of the Army of the Valley," *Military Affairs* 12 (1948), 227–28; Francis G. Ruffin to Major Hawks, February 21, 1862, Hawks Papers.

9. Tanner, *Stonewall in the Valley*, 100–101, 104; Montague, "Subsistence of the Army of the Valley," 228; *O.R.* 5, 1086; *O.R.* 51, pt. 2, 534.

10. Entry for March 11, 1862, in the Diary of Laura Lee, Swem Library, College of William and Mary, Williamsburg, Virginia; Tanner, *Stonewall in the Valley*, 108–10; Douglas Southall Freeman, *Lee's Lieutenants* (New York: Charles Scribner's Sons, 1942–44), vol. 1, 311.

11. Chase Diary, March 9, 1862; Griffith Diary, note 74; McDonald Diary, 40.

12. Entry for March 12, 1862, in the Journal of John Peyton Clarke, from the Louisa Crawford Collection, Winchester-Frederick County Historical Society Archives, Winchester, Virginia; Laura Lee Diary, March 12, 1862; Brooke Journal, March 12, 1862.

13. Clarke Journal, March 12, 1862; Laura Lee Diary, March 12, 1862.

14. Entries for March 15 and 17, 1862, in the Mrs. Hugh Lee Diary, March 1862–November 1865, Mrs. Hugh Lee Collection, Winchester-Frederick County Historical Society Archives, Winchester, Virginia; McDonald Diary, 42, 44, 46–48, 50–51; Laura Lee Diary, March 13 and 14, 1862; Clarke Journal, March 12, 18, 19, 25, 1862.

15. McDonald Diary, 50.

16. Laura Lee Diary, March 14, 1862; Mrs. Hugh Lee Diary, March 16, 1862; Chase Diary, March 23, 1862.

17. Chase Diary, March 10, 11, 17, April 6, 13, 16, 24, 1862; Griffith Diary, 72–74.

18. McKown Diary, February 16 and 19, March 18, 1862; Treadwell Smith Diary, April 7, 9, 15, 22, 26–28, 1862; Anna Andrews to Courtney B. Jones, April 27, 1862, Andrews Papers; Clarke Journal, March 24, April 15, 1862.

19. Clarke Journal, March 12, 1862; Laura Lee Diary, March 13, 1862; Mrs. Hugh Lee Diary, March 13, 1862; Chase Diary, March 12, 1862; Griffith Diary, 76–78.

20. Griffith Diary, 78; Laura Lee Diary, April 24, 1862; Clarke Journal, March 12 and 31, 1862; Chase Diary, March 17, April 6, 1862; Brooke Journal, April 5, 1862.

21. Treadwell Smith Diary, March 10, 23–24, 28, April 1, 1862; Laura Lee Diary, March 13, 1862; Clarke Journal, March 15 and 21, 1862; McDonald Diary, 43–45.

22. McDonald Diary, 44–45; Clarke Journal, March 12–13, 20, 1862; Laura Lee Diary, March 14, 1862.

23. Clarke Journal, March 14–17, 19, 28, April 2, 4–5, 17, 23, 1862; Mrs. Hugh Lee Diary, March 21, 1862; Laura Lee Diary, April 1 and 17, May 5, 1862.

24. Clarke Journal, March 28, April 16 and 17, May 17, 1862; entry for May 19, 1862, in the Diary of Matthella Page Harrison, Special Collections, Alderman Library, University of Virginia, Charlottesville, Virginia; Treadwell Smith Diary, March 4, 1862; Anna Andrews to My Dear Sister, April 27, 1862, Andrews Papers; McKown Diary, March 18 and 30, 1862.

25. Jane L. Buck to My Dear Richard, May 27, 1862, Richard B. Buck Collection; Clarke Journal, March 15 and 20, 1862; Mrs. Hugh Lee Diary, March 21, 1862; Laura Lee Diary, March 22, April 14, 17, 21, 23, 27, May 5, 1862.

26. Laura Lee Diary, March 22, April 14 and 21, 1862; Jane L. Buck to My Dear Richard, May 27, 1862, Richard B. Buck Collection; Clarke Journal, March 15, 1862; Anna Andrews to My Dear Sister, April 27, 1862, Andrews Papers; Brooke Journal, March 17, 1862; Clarke Journal, March 15, 1862; Laura Lee Diary, April 14, 1862.

27. Laura Lee Diary, April 4, 1862; Clarke Journal, March 20, 1862; Ashby, *The Valley Campaigns*, 73; A. B. Rober to My Dear Cousin, April 29, 1862, James M. Schreckhire Papers, Special Collections, Duke University Library, Durham, North Carolina; C. G. Marchais to Capt. Edmondson, March 16, 1862, Edmondson Correspondence; Preston Diary, April 3, 1862.

28. Clarke Journal, April 20, 1862; Ashby, *The Valley Campaigns*, 73; *O.R.* 51, pt. 2, 550–51; Frank Paxton to his wife, April 1, 1862, Paxton, *Civil War Letters*, 45; *Lexington Gazette*, April 10, 1862; A. B. Rober to My Dear Cousin, April 29, 1862, Schreckhire Papers.

29. McFarland Diary, 88–89; William Hooke to his son, February 10, 1862, Hooke Papers; G. G. Schreckhire to his son, March 5, 1862; A. B. Rober to My Dear Cousin, April 29, 1862, Schreckhire Papers; *Lexington Gazette*, May 8, November 29, 1862.

30. *O.R.* 51, pt. 2, 495; ibid. 5, 1097.

31. Ibid., 12, pt. 3, 835; Reuben to Mollie, March 24, 1862, Burress Collection; James J. White to Dear Colonel, March 3, 1862, *Letters of James J. White.*

32. Roll of Company D, 33rd Virginia Regiment, Frederick William Mackey Holliday Papers, Special Collections, Duke University Library, Durham, North Carolina; J. H. Langhorne to his mother, January 12, 1862; G. K. Harlow to his wife, January 23, 1862, both quoted in Tanner, *Stonewall in the Valley*, 91; Haywood to Dear Father, February 17, 1862, Haywood and W. D. Hardy Papers, Special Collections, Duke University Library, Durham, North Carolina.

33. *O.R.* 5, 1016.

34. Freeman, *R. E. Lee*, vol. 2, 26; Tanner, *Stonewall in the Valley*, 92–93; *O.R.* 6, 350.

35. *O.R.* series IV, vol. 1, 1031.

36. Ibid., series IV, vol. 1, 1095–1100; *Staunton Spectator*, April 15, 1862.

37. *O.R.* series IV, vol. 1, 1011–12, 1114–15; *Staunton Spectator*, March 4, 1862.

38. JBD To Dear Greenlee, February 7, 1862, Dorman Papers; G. G. Schreckhire to Dear Son, March 5, 1862, Schreckhire Papers; William Hooke to Dear Franklin, February 10, 1862; William Hooke to Dear Friend, February 28, 1862, Hooke Papers; Guy F. Hershberger, "Mennonites in the Civil War," *Mennonite Quarterly Review*, 18 (1948), 140–41; Reuben to Mollie, March 19 and 21, 1862, Burress Collection; E. C. Marchais to Capt. Edmondson, March 16, 1862; J. K. Edmondson to My Dear Wife, April 3 and 14, 1862, Edmondson Correspondence; *O.R.* 12, pt. 3, 835, 841.

39. McPherson, *Battle Cry of Freedom*, 432; Ashby, *The Valley Campaigns*, 84; Preston Diary, April 3, 1862; McFarland Diary, March 8 and 12, 1862; William Hooke to Dear Franklin, March 9, 1862, Hooke Papers; Your Sister Liz to Dear John, March 4, 1862, Harris Papers, Placed on deposit by the Harrisonburg-Rockingham County Historical Society; Reuben to Mollie, April 17, 1862, Burress Collection.

40. McPherson, *Battle Cry of Freedom*, 456–60; James McPherson, *Ordeal by Fire: The Civil War and Reconstruction* (New York: Alfred A. Knopf, 1982), 239–42; Bruce Catton, *Terrible Swift Sword* (New York: Doubleday and Company, 1963), 300–305.

41. McFarland Diary, April 29, May 9, June 9, 1862; entry for June 7, 1862, in the Diary of Nancy Emerson, Special Collections, Alderman Library, University of Virginia, Charlottesville, Virginia; Harrison Diary, May 25, 1862; Mrs. Hugh Lee Diary, May 24 and 31, 1862; Buck Diary, May 7, 1862; Preston Diary, June 3, 1862.

42. Brooke Journal, June 7, 9, 10, 1862; Clarke Journal, May 17, 1862; Harrison Diary, June 6 and 11, 1862; Treadwell Smith Diary, June 16 and 18, 1862; Jane L. Buck to Dear Richard, May 27, 1862, Richard B. Buck Collection; Buck Diary, May 14 and 18, July 1, 1862.

43. J: K. Edmondson to My Dear Wife, May 26, 1862, Edmondson Correspondence; Mrs. Hugh Lee Diary, May 27, 1862; McDonald Diary, 68–69; Harrison Diary, May 31, 1862; Emerson Diary, June 8, 1862; Elizabeth Preston Allan, *The Life and Letters of Margaret Junkin Preston* (New York: Houghton, Mifflin, 1903), May 27, 1862 (hereafter cited as Preston Diary); Brooke Journal, June 14, 1862.

44. Preston Diary, May 27, 1862; Mrs. Hugh Lee Diary, May 27, 1862.

45. *O.R.* 5, 836, 977, 1011, 1067; ibid. series IV, vol. 1, 876–77.

46. *Lexington Gazette*, May 15, 1862.

47. *O.R.* 51, pt. 2, 550–51, 587–88.

48. Ibid., 5, 1084.

49. Ibid., 11, pt. 3, 512–13; Montague, "Subsistence of the Army of the Valley," 228–31; Statement of Return of Provisions, Received and Issued at ————, for the months of March, April, and a partial return of June, 1862, Hawks Papers.

50. L. B. Northrop to Major Hawks, July 3, 1862; J. H. Clairbourne to Major, August 2, 1862; L. B. Northrop to Major, August 7, 1862; P. Williams to Major, August 23 and 25, September 1, 1862. All letters in Hawks Papers.

51. Monthly Statement of Funds Received and Disbursed at ————, for the months of July, August, September, October, and November; totals of receipts of provisions purchased or received between July 1 and November 30, 1862; J. M. Galt to Major, August 7, 8, 12, 22, 30, 1862; Geo. Kearsley to Major, September 8, 1862, Hawks Papers.

52. McFarland Diary, August 18 and 19, 1862; Joe Dinwiddie to Maj. Wm. Hawks, August 12, 1862, Maj. P. Williams to Major, August 23 and 25, September 1, 1862, all letters in Hawks Papers; *Lexington Gazette*, August 7, 1862; *Staunton Spectator*, October 21, 1862; F. N. Boney, *John Letcher of Virginia: The Story of Virginia's Civil War Governor* (Tuscaloosa: University of Alabama Press, 1966), 175; *O.R.* 19, pt. 2, 699–700, 702.

53. Freeman, *R. E. Lee*, vol. 2, 405–6, 415–16.

54. McKown Diary, October 25 and 26, 1862; Treadwell Smith Diary, November 14, 1862; Statement of Damage, submitted by William Abbott of Frederick County, due to the occupancy of his lands by Confederate Troops, October 27, 1862, William Abbott Papers, Special Collections,

Duke University Library, Durham, North Carolina; Treadwell Smith Diary, September 23, October 15 and 31, November 9, 11, 14, 1862; Margaret A. Russell to Mr. Philip Williams, November 18, 1862, Philip Williams Family Correspondence, The Handley Library, Winchester, Virginia.

55. James Steptoe to Mary Green, September 29, 1862, Family Correspondence, Mercer G. Johnston Papers, Manuscript Division, Library of Congress, Washington, D.C.

56. Jedediah Hotchkiss to My Dear Brother, September 28, 1862, Family Correspondence, Jedediah Hotchkiss Papers, Manuscript Division, Library of Congress, Washington, D.C.; Margaret A. Russell to Mr. Philip Williams, November 18, 1862, Philip Williams Family Correspondence; O.R. 19, pt. 2, 673.

57. Harrison Diary, September 25, 1862; A. C. R. Jones to unknown, October 28, 1862, Ann Cary Randolph Jones Family Papers, The Handley Library, Winchester, Virginia; Buck Diary, September 2 and 23, 1862; Preston Diary, September 11, 1862; Chase Diary, September 20, 1862; Laura Lee Diary, September 20, 1862; McDonald Diary, 88–90; Buck Diary, August 31, September 2 and 7, 1862; William S. White, *Rev. William S. White and His Times: An Autobiography*, edited by Rev. H. M. White (Richmond, Va.: Presbyterian Committee of Publication, 1891), 177–79; Preston Diary, September 3, 6, 11, 1862; McDonald Diary, October 21, 1862.

58. Chase Diary, May 24, 25, 27, June 4 and 5, July 26, August 15, 25, 27, 28, September 1, 3, 8, 9, 1862; John E. Fleming to Honorable W. T. Willey, May 16, 1862; R. A. Sommerville to Dear Sir, July 12, 1862, Willey Papers; Diary of a Southern Sympathizer, 1862–1865, author unknown, May 25 and 31, 1862, West Virginia and Regional History Collection, WVU Libraries; Sperow Daybook, November 11, 1862; Laura Lee Diary, July 24, 26, 28, 30, August 6 and 28, 1862; Treadwell Smith Diary, June 7, 16, 18, August 8 and 9, 1862; D. N. Kees to Mr. J. M. Cambel [*sic*], June 29, 1862, Jane Hedges to Dear Sir, August 9, 1862, Jacob M. Campbell Papers, West Virginia and Regional History Collection, WVU Libraries; Clarke Journal, June 9, August 18, September 16, 1862; Brooke Journal, June 9, 10, 15, August 15 and 20, 1862.

59. O.R. 12, pt. 2, 52; Chase Diary, June 5, July 22, 1862; Diary of a Southern Sympathizer, October 24, 1862; Laura Lee Diary, July 22, August 22 and 24, 1862; Brooke Journal, August 15, 1862; Clarke Journal, July 28, September 1, 1862.

60. Harrison Diary, September 17, 1862; Chase Diary, September 29, October 4, 11, 28, November 15, 1862; George to Dear Sister, November 6, 1862, McGuffin Family Papers; Your Father to Dear Greenlee, October 13, 1862, Davidson Papers, WLU; Frank to his wife, November 11, 1862, Paxton, *Civil War Letters*, 63; *Lexington Gazette*, October 9, 1862; Jennie Daugherty to Dear Mother, November 24, 1862, Jackson-Trout Papers; Preston Diary, October 23, 1862; Your Father to Dear Greenlee, October 13, 1862, Davidson Papers, WLU.

61. *Lexington Gazette*, October 9, November 13, 1862; *Rockingham Register*, November 14, 1862; *Staunton Spectator*, October 21 and 28, November 4, December 16, 1862.

62. W. Frazier to My Dear Sir, November 13, 1862, Davidson Papers, WLU; *Lexington Gazette*, June 12, October 2, 23, 30, November 6 and 13, 1862; *Staunton Spectator*, April 8, October 28, December 16, 1862.

63. *O.R.* 19, pt. 2, 659, 663.

64. Diary of Jedediah Hotchkiss, October 19 and 24, 1862, Jedediah Hotchkiss Papers, Manuscript Division, Library of Congress, Washington, D.C.; Preston Diary, October 23, 1862; *Lexington Gazette*, October 30, 1862; Your Father to Dear Greenlee, October 13, 1862, Davidson Papers, WLU; *O.R.* 21, 1025; *O.R.* series IV, vol. 2, 158.

65. *O.R.* series IV, vol. 2, 158; *Lexington Gazette*, May 1 and 8, October 9, 23, 30, November 13, 1862; *Rockingham Register*, November 14, 1862; *Staunton Spectator*, November 4, 1862; Jedediah Hotchkiss to Nelson, November 12, 1862, Family Correspondence, Hotchkiss Papers.

66. *O.R.* series IV, vol. 2, 158–59, 193; Francis G. Ruffin, "A Chapter in Confederate History," *North American Review*, 30 (1882), 100–101.

67. *Rockingham Register, November 14, 1862, December 19, 1862;* Staunton Spectator, November 4, 1862; Margaret A. Russell to Philip Williams, November 18, 1862, Philip Williams Family Correspondence; *O.R.* series IV, vol. 2, 159, 192.

68. *O.R.* 19, pt. 2, 640–42.

69. Testimony of Francis G. Ruffin before the Joint Committee on Quartermaster and Commissaries of the Confederate Congress concerning the Confederate States Subsistence Department, January 20, 1865, Francis G. Ruffin Papers, Virginia Historical Society, Richmond, Virginia; *O.R.* 51, pt. 2, 674–75.

70. Preston Diary, December 24, 1862; Laura Lee Diary, December 31, 1862.

CHAPTER 5: "ALAS! WHEN IS THE END TO BE?"

1. Harrison Diary, January 5 and 26, February 2, 26, 1863; Diary of a Southern Sympathizer, January 12 and 16, 1862; Unsigned to Dear Frederick, January 9, 1862, Holiday Papers; McDonald Diary, January 1 and 9, 1863; A. C. R. Jones to unaddressed, December 4, 1862, Ann Cary Randolph Jones Family Papers; Treadwell Smith Diary, December 27, 1862, January 3, 1863; *O.R.* series III, vol. 3, 13–14; Harrison Diary, January 17 and 26, February 17, 21, 25, 28, 1863; Buck Diary, January 12–14, 1863; William L. Wilson, *Borderline Confederate*, edited by Festus P. Summers (Pittsburgh, Pa.: University of Pittsburgh Press, 1962), 44–45, 48–49.

2. Laura Lee Diary, January 7, 20, 21, February 1, 6, 9, 11, 25, 28, March 11, 1863; Chase Diary, January 28, 1863; Harrison Diary, February 28, 21, 25, 28, March 19, 28, 30, April 3 and 6, 1863; Your Margaret to My Dear Own One, March 24, 1863, Philip Williams Family Correspondence; Treadwell Smith Diary, March 3 and 7, 1863; McDonald Diary, January 12, February 2, 1863.

3. Garland R. Quarles, *Occupied Winchester, 1861–1865* (Winchester, Va.: Farmers and Merchants Banks, 1976), 81; Laura Lee Diary, January 1 and 3, April 9, 1863; McDonald Diary, February 2, 1863.

4. Mrs. Hugh Lee Diary, January 19, February 19, 20, 23, 1863; McDonald Diary, January 21, February 2, 3, 20, 1863; Laura Lee Diary, January 17 and 31, April 4, 1863.

5. Laura Lee Diary, January 17, February 20, April 4, 1863; Mrs. Hugh Lee Diary, January 10, February 19 and 23, 1863; McDonald Diary, February 20 and 27, March 1, 1863; Quarles, *Occupied Winchester*, 83.

6. Laura Lee Diary, February 20, 23, 25, 27, 28, March 16, April 4, 1863; Mrs. Hugh Lee Diary, January 19, February 19, 20, 23, 24, 1863.

7. McDonald Diary, January 10, 1863; Quarles, *Occupied Winchester*, 83–84; Laura Lee Diary, January 19 and 29, March 16–18, April 7 and 9, 1863; Mrs. Hugh Lee Diary, March 16, 1863.

8. A. C. R. Jones to unaddressed, June 6, 1863, Ann Cary Randolph Jones Family Papers; Mrs. Hugh Lee Diary, January 3, February 13 and 22, 1863; Laura Lee Diary, January 3 and 17, February 6, March 9, 19, 26, April 6, 1863; Portia Baldwin Baker Diary, January 1, 1863, Winchester-Frederick County Historical Society Archives, Winchester, Virginia; McDonald Diary, January 8, 9, 20, April 9, 1863.

9. Harrison Diary, February 18, 1863; *O.R.* 25, pt. 2, 604; *O.R.* 51, pt. 2, 677–78; *O.R.* series III, vol. 3, 13.

10. *O.R.* 21, 1092; ibid. 25, pt. 2, 604–5; Wilson, *Borderline Confederate*, 43–45, 48, 50, 53.

11. *O.R.* 21, 1110; ibid. 25, pt. 2, 597–98.

12. *O.R.* 21, 1080; ibid. 51, pt. 2, 676.

13. Ibid., 25, pt. 2, 598, 652–53, 659, 679, 684–85, 693, 710–12, 743, 819–20; ibid. 27, pt. 2, 924.

14. Ibid., 18, 859, 874; ibid. 21, 1110; ibid. 23, pt. 2, 626; ibid. 25, pt. 2, 612, 730; ibid. 51, pt. 2, 674–75; ibid. series IV, vol. 2, 350–51.

15. Angus J. Johnston, *Virginia Railroads in the Civil War* (Chapel Hill: University of North Carolina Press, 1961), 11; *O.R.* 5, 875–76.

16. Turner, "The Virginia Central Railroad at War," 521.

17. Ibid., 523–24, 528–29; *O.R.* 51, pt. 2, 678.

18. *O.R.* 21, 1110; ibid. 23, pt. 2, 626; ibid. 25, pt. 2, 686–87, 725, 730; Goff, *Confederate Supply*, 74.

19. *O.R.* series IV, vol. 2, 457; ibid. 25, pt. 2, 693, 735–36.

20. Ibid., series IV, vol. 2, 475–77.

21. *Lexington Gazette*, April 15, 1863; *Staunton Spectator*, April 21, 1863; McPherson, *Battle Cry of Freedom*, 640–45; Catton, *Glory Road* (Garden City, N.Y.: Doubleday, 1952), 184–88; Freeman, *Lee's Lieutenants*, vol. 2, 546–59.

22. Freeman, *Lee's Lieutenants*, vol. 2, 669–70, 680–82; Foote, *The Civil War*, vol. 2, 300–302.

23. McDonald Diary, May 8, 13, 15, 1863; Mrs. Hugh Lee Diary, May 13–15, 1863; unaddressed and unsigned letter, May 15, 1863, Ann Cary Randolph Jones Family Papers; McFarland Diary, May 13, 1863; Preston Diary, May 12, 1863; Laura Lee Diary, May 14, 1863; Buck Diary, May 13 and 15, 1863; Chase Diary, May 7, 1863.

24. Harrison Diary, April 3, 6, 20, May 15, 25, 27, June 11, 1863; M.B.B. to Dear Richard, May 3, 1863, Richard B. Buck Collection; Buck Diary, May 16 and 17, 1863.

25. McDonald Diary, April 7, 14, 19, May 3, 15, 22, June 4 and 9, 1863; Mrs. Hugh Lee Diary, April 6–8, 1863; Laura Lee Diary, April 7, 8, 16, May 18 and 20, June 10, 1863; Chase Diary, June 10, 1863.

26. William C. Davis, *Jefferson Davis: The Man and His Hour* (New York: HarperCollins, 1991), 504–5; Bruce Catton, *Never Call Retreat* (Garden City, N.Y.: Doubleday, 1965), 161–63; Freeman, *Lee's Lieutenants*, vol. 3, 20–27; *O.R.* 27, pt. 2, 305.

27. Mrs. Hugh Lee Diary, June 14 and 15, 1863; McDonald Diary, June 14–16, 1863; Laura Lee Diary, June 14–16, 1863.

28. McDonald Diary, June 16, 1863; Laura Lee Diary, June 16, 1863; Mrs. Hugh Lee Diary, June 16, 1863; Freeman, *Lee's Lieutenants*, vol. 3, 26.

29. McPherson, *Battle Cry of Freedom*, 653–62; Catton, *Never Call Retreat*, 178–91; Freeman, *R. E. Lee*, vol. 3, 68–71, 118–28.

30. John D. Imboden, "The Confederate Retreat from Gettysburg," in *Battles and Leaders of the Civil War*, edited by Robert U. Johnson and Clarence B. Buel (reprint, New York: Thomas Yoseloff, 1956), vol. 3, 422–26; *O.R.* 27, pt. 2, 346; Freeman, *R. E. Lee*, vol. 3, 136–37, 141, 144; Chase Diary, July 21, 1863; McKown Diary, July 16, 20–23, 1863.

31. McKown Diary, July 15–20, 22, 23, 1863; Harrison Diary, July 20, 1863.

32. McKown Diary, July 7 and 9, 1863; Chase Diary, May 9, 14, 22, July 7, 13, 17–18, 1863; McDonald Diary, May 15, 1863; Laura Lee Diary, May 12, 16, 19, July 7, 1863; *O.R.* 27, pt. 3, 916.

33. McKown Diary, June 26, 1863; Chase Diary, July 10, 1863; Laura Lee Diary, July 7, 1863; Preston Diary, July 7 and 11, 1863; M. B. Buck to My Very Dear Son, June 24, 1863, Richard B. Buck Collection; Buck Diary, June 22–24, July 6, 10, 12, 1863; Diary of Frank M. Imboden, July 31, 1863, Frank Imboden Collection, Special Collections, Alderman Library, University of Virginia, Charlottesville, Virginia; Laura Lee Diary, July 29, 1863.

34. Laura Lee Diary, July 29, 1863; Chase Diary, July 24, 1863; A. C. R. Jones to unaddressed, August 7, 1863, Ann Cary Randolph Jones Family Papers; Mrs. Hugh Lee Diary, August 6, 1863; Harrison Diary, undated July 1863 entry.

35. Chase Diary, July 24, 1863; Laura Lee Diary, July 29, 1863; A. C. R. Jones to unaddressed, August 6, 1863, Ann Cary Randolph Jones Family Papers; McDonald Diary, 177–79; Mrs. Hugh Lee Diary, August 20, September 20, 1863.

36. Chase Diary, November 9, December 2, 1862; Wilson, *Borderline Confederate*, 49; Laura Lee Diary, July 29, 1863; Preston Diary, April 14, July 1, 1863.

37. *O.R.* 27, pt. 3, 1049; ibid. 29, pt. 2, 623, 650–51, 814, 889–90; ibid. 51, pt. 2, 807; Frank Imboden Diary, July 14 and 22, 1863; Freeman, *R. E. Lee*, vol. 3, 144.

38. Marcus B. Buck to Dear Richard, May 3, 1863, Richard B. Buck Collection; *O.R.* 27, pt. 3, 1049; Petition of James Sterrett, Davidson Papers, WSHS; McDonald Diary, 180, footnote; Josephine Forney Roedel Diary, 393–94, Manuscript Division, Library of Congress, Washington, D.C.; McPherson, *Ordeal by Fire*, 182; J. D. Davidson to Dear Sir, November 1, 1863, Davidson Papers, WSHS; Ruffin, "A Chapter in Confederate History," 108.

39. U.S. Government: *The Eighth Census of the United States, Volume On Agriculture*, 155, 158, 162; J. D. Davidson to My Dear Sir, August 27, 1861, Davidson Papers, Duke University; Margaret A. Russell to Mr. Philip Williams, November 18, 1862, Philip Williams Family Correspondence; R.B.B. to Marcus Buck, January 29, February 1 and 6, 1862, Richard B. Buck Transcripts; Reuben to Dear Pa, April 17, 1862, Burress Collection; Your Sister Liz to Dear John, March 4, 1862, Harris Papers, placed on deposit by the Harrisonburg-Rockingham County Historical Society; Your Father to Dear William, February 10, 1862, Wm. Hooke to Dear Franklin, March 9, 1862, Hooke Papers; George Baylor to Mary Baylor, November 6, 1862, McGuffin Family Papers.

40. Treadwell Smith Diary, January 26, August 7, September 9, 1863; Buck Diary, January 13 and 15, May 17, July 24, October 27, 1863; McKown Diary, February 7 and 10, August 22, September 25 and 29, December 6, 1863; Harrison Diary, March 2 and 18, 1863; Your Margaret to My Own Dear One, March 24, 1863, Philip Williams Family Correspondence; Pitman Diary, December 4, 1863; *Staunton Spectator*, August 4, December 8, 1863; *Rockingham Register*, June 5, 1863; Chase Diary, August 6, 1863; McPherson, *Ordeal by Fire*, 169.

41. *O.R.* 29, pt. 2, 656; C.S.A. War Department, "Communication from the Secretary of War," (transmitting a report by the assistant quartermaster general in charge of the tax-in-kind, Larkin Smith), January 19, 1864, note 6, Rare Book Room, Library of Congress, Washington, D.C.; Fontaine W. Mahood, "A History of the Commissary Department," 4, Virginia Historical Society, Richmond, Virginia; Ruffin, "A Chapter in Confederate History," 108; McKown Diary, June 15–August 15, 1863; McFarland Diary, 92–93.

42. Ruffin, "A Chapter in Confederate History," 106–7; Robert Garlick Hill Kean, *Inside the Confederate Government: The Diary of Robert Garlick Hill Kean*, edited by Edward Younger (New York: Oxford University Press, 1957), 41; *O.R.* 25, pt. 2, 666; *Lexington Gazette*, January 29, 1863; *Staunton Spectator*, March 3, 1863.

43. McPherson, *Ordeal by Fire*, 378; *O.R.* series IV, vol. 2, 559, 652, 843; Paul Escott, *After Secession: Jefferson Davis and the Failure of Confederate Nationalism* (Baton Rouge: Louisiana State University Press, 1978), 68–69.

44. Ruffin, "A Chapter in Confederate History," 104, 106; J. D. Davidson to Dear Sir, November 1, 1863, Davidson Papers, WSHS; *Staunton Spectator*, October 13, 20, 27, November 24, 1863; Unsigned to My Dear Sir, November 22, 1863, Davidson Papers, WSHS.

45. C.S.A. Executive Department, Treasury Department, 1863 Tax-in-Kind Estimates for Albemarle County, Amherst County, Buckingham County, Fluvanna County, and Nelson County, Virginia, Special Collections, Duke University Library, Durham, North Carolina.

46. C.S.A. War Department, "Communication from the Secretary of War," tax-in-kind report; Ruffin, "A Chapter in Confederate History," 106–7; *O.R.* series IV, vol. 2, 960, 968.

47. Buck Diary, October 6, 1863; *Lexington Gazette*, November 18, 1863; J. D. Davidson to My Dear Sir, November 1, 1863, J. D. Davidson to Dear Governor, November 6, 1863, Davidson Papers, WSHS; Mary to My Dear Papa, December 8, 1863, Pendleton Papers; Your Daughter to My Dear Mother, September 15, 1863, Jackson-Trout Papers; McPherson, *Ordeal by Fire*, 377; Mrs. Hugh Lee Diary, August 5, 1863; J. D. Davidson to My Dear Sir, November 1, 1863, Davidson Papers, WSHS; Your Loving Mary to James J. White, November 12, 1863, Reid-White Papers; Mary to My Dear Papa, December 8, 1863, Pendleton Papers; *Staunton Spectator*, October 27, 1863; Preston Diary, November 16, December 4, 1863.

48. Alexander H. H. Stuart to Dear Davidson, December 15, 1863, Davidson Papers, WSHS.

49. Mrs. Hugh Lee Diary, August 1 and 5, November 9, 1863; Laura Lee Diary, October 20 and 28, November 9 and 17, December 6 and 22, 1863; Chase Diary, August 13, 17, 22, September 1, 8, 13, 18, 19, 25, 28, October 13, 15, 19, 20, November 1, 4, 21, December 11, 16, 17, 1863; Preston Diary, November 6, 8–11, December 6 and 20, 1863; Alexander H. H. Stuart to Dear Davidson, December 15, 1863, Davidson Papers, WSHS; Your Loving Mary to James J. White, November 12, 1863, Reid-White Papers.

CHAPTER 6: "THERE IS NOT SUFFICIENT IN THE VALLEY TO LIVE OFF THE COUNTRY"

1. McDonald Diary, 198, 200; *Lexington Gazette*, January 13 and 27, 1864; Preston Diary, January 2, 1864; M.B.B. to Dear Richard, February 27, 1864, M. B. Buck to Dear Richard, April 19, 1864, Richard B. Buck Collection; Jed. Hotchkiss to My Dear Brother, January 24, 1864, Hotchkiss Papers.

2. Jed. Hotchkiss to My Dear Brother, January 24, 1864, Hotchkiss Papers; *Lexington Gazette*, April 14, May 11, 1864; McFarland Diary, February 3 and 25, 1864; Preston Diary, February 19, 26, 29, 1864.

3. Pitman Diary, February 26, March 23, 1864; McPherson, *Ordeal by Fire*, 182; *Staunton Spectator*, February 9, 1864; *Lexington Gazette*, February 10, 1864; *Rockingham Register*, editorial reprinted in the *Lexington Gazette*, February 10, 1864.

4. Confederate States of America, Army Record Book, 1864–1865, Lists of Exemptions, Reserves, and Substitutes in Rockbridge County, Rockbridge Historical Society, The University Library, Washington and Lee University, Lexington, Virginia; Petition from Citizens of Shenandoah County, Virginia, received March 7, 1864, Jno. L. Calvert to His Excellency Jefferson Davis, March 7, 1864, William G. Thompson Papers, Special Collections, Duke University Library, Durham, North Carolina.

5. John T. Harris to Hon. J. B. Baldwin, March 14, 1864, W. F. to John T. Harris, Esq., April 18, 1864, Harris Papers, placed on deposit by the Harrisonburg-Rockingham County Historical Society; Petitions of John Wilson, Elis Tutwiller, John M. Yoville, Charles B. McClung, John B. Dryden, James R. Sterrett, John M. Humphries, February, May, undated, 1864, Issac C. C. Moore to Mr. Jas. D. Davidson, February 3, 1864, L. Bassett French to W. C. Lewis, Esq., February 18, 1864, I. C. Moore to Mr. Davidson, February 19, 1864, Davidson Papers, WSHS.

6. Chase Diary, January 15, 16, 22, 1864; Laura Lee Diary, January 16 and 19, 1864.

7. Laura Lee Diary, January 23, 25, 27, 29, 1864; Chase Diary, January 18, 19, 22, 23, 30, 1864.

8. Laura Lee Diary, February 10, 1864; Preston Diary, February 10, 1864; *Staunton Spectator*, February 9, 1864; *Lexington Gazette*, February 17, April 20, 1864.

9. *O.R.* 33, 1114.

10. Ruffin, "A Chapter in Confederate History," 107–8; *O.R.* 33, 1059, 1101, 1112–13, 1139–40, 1159, 1166; *O.R.* 51, pt. 2, 853.

11. *O.R.* 33, 1134, 1194–95; William N. McDonald, *A History of the Laurel Brigade* (Baltimore: Sun Job Printing Office, 1907), 223; Mahood, "A History of the Commissary Department," 37; McDonald Diary, 199.

12. *Staunton Spectator*, March 8, 1864; *Lexington Gazette*, April 6, 13, 1864.

13. *O.R.* series IV, vol. 3, 88–89; ibid. 33, 1077; ibid. 51, pt. 2, 808; ibid. 32, pt. 3, 598; Hawks Papers, box 8.

14. *O.R.* 33, 1178, 1236–37; ibid. 52, pt. 2, 660; ibid. 32, pt. 2, 762.

15. *O.R.* 51, pt. 2, 808, 850–51; ibid. series IV, vol. 3, 88–89; Statement of Maj. A. M. Allen, January 19, 1864, Statement of Col. R. S. Cole, February 8, 1864, Confederate States of America Papers, War Department, Subsistence Department Letterbooks, January 2, 1864–December 31, 1864, Virginia Historical Society, Richmond, Virginia.

16. *O.R.* 25, pt. 2, 683–84; ibid. 29, pt. 2, 832–33; ibid. 18, 825; ibid. 51, pt. 2, 747, 798; Johnston, *Virginia Railroads in the Civil War*, 128, 176; Turner, "The Virginia Central Railroad at War," 530.

17. *O.R.* 33, 1073, 1275; ibid. 40, pt. 2, 697–98; ibid. 51, pt. 2, 903; ibid. series IV, vol. 3, 226, 228; Statement of Colonel R. S. Cole, February 8, 1864, Subsistence Department Letterbooks; Turner, "The Virginia Central Railroad at War," 531–32.

18. Bruce Catton, *Grant Takes Command* (Boston: Little, Brown, 1968), 142, 152, 250–51, 277–79.

19. Laura Lee Diary, April 12 and 20, May 2, 4–7, 1864; Mrs. Hugh Lee Diary, May 5 and 6, 1864; Chase Diary, May 1 and 9, 1864.

20. Preston Diary, May 10, 1864; Freeman, *Lee's Lieutenants*, vol. 3, 515; Catton, *Never Call Retreat*, 352–53.

21. Chase Diary, May 16 and 17, 1864; Foote, *The Civil War*, vol. 3, 248–49; Catton, *Never Call Retreat*, 352–53.

22. *O.R.* 37, pt. 1, 94–95, 492–93, 500, 507, 517–18; Catton, *A Stillness at Appomattox*, 178; Freeman, *Lee's Lieutenants*, vol. 3, 516; McPherson, *Battle Cry of Freedom*, 737.

23. *O.R.* 37, pt. 1, 518, 543; McPherson, *Battle Cry of Freedom*, 737–38; Diary of William Patterson, May 20, 27–30, June 2, 9, 12, 16, 1864, Southern Historical Collection, Wilson Library, University of North Carolina, Chapel Hill; Diary of Frank Smith Reader, May 23–24, 27–29, June 1, 1864, University Library, Washington and Lee University, Lexington, Virginia.

24. Pitman Diary, May 26 and 28, 1864; McFarland Diary, June 8 and 9, 1864; Laura Lee Diary, May 26 and 28, June 2 and 6, 1864; Chase Diary, May 26, 1864; E. B. Pendleton to Dear Sir, June 6, 1864, Willey Papers; Preston Diary, June 3, 6–9, 11, 1864; Emerson Diary, July 9, 13, 19, 21, 1864.

25. Lucas P. Thompson to Dear Sir, July 1, 1864, undated and unsigned letter, Davidson Papers, WSHS; McDonald Diary, June 1864, 210–20; William S. White to My Dear Brother, July 6, 1864, Francis McFarland Collection; Preston Diary, June 11–14, 16–17, 1864; White Diary, 185–90.

26. Boney, *John Letcher of Virginia*, 205–8; Preston Diary, June 12–14, 16, 1864; William S. White to My Dear Brother, July 6, 1864, Francis McFarland Collection; White Diary, 185–87; McDonald Diary, June 1864, 206–8; *O.R.* 37, pt. 1, 97; Lucas P. Thompson to My Dear Sir, July 1, 1864, Davidson Papers, WSHS.

27. Freeman, *Lee's Lieutenants*, vol. 3, 516, 523–27; Catton, *Grant Takes Command*, 298–300; *O.R.* 37, pt. 1, 97–101.

28. *O.R.* 37, pt. 1, 347–49, 767; Harrison Diary, July 2, 1864; Laura Lee Diary, July 4, 1864; Chase Diary, July 2, 1864; Freeman, *Lee's Lieutenants*, vol. 3, 557, 559, 565–76.

29. *O.R.* 43, pt. 1, 1021–22; ibid. 37, pt. 1, 337, 355; Freeman, *Lee's Lieutenants*, vol. 3, 570–72; Catton, *Grant Takes Command*, 342–43, 346.

30. Catton, *Grant Takes Command*, 342–43; Philip H. Sheridan, *Personal Memoirs of P. H. Sheridan* (New York: Charles L. Webster, 1888), vol. 1, 464–65; *O.R.* 43, pt. 1, 695, 719, 917.

31. Wert, *From Winchester to Cedar Creek*, 29; James H. Wilson, *Under the Old Flag* (reprint, Westport, Conn.: Greenwood Press, 1971), vol. 2, 548; Freeman, *Lee's Lieutenants*, vol. 3, 576–77, 581.

32. Treadwell Smith Diary, August 10, 14, 25, 1864; Diary of a Southern Sympathizer, August 28, 1864; McKown Diary, September 4 and 9, 1864; Laura Lee Diary, September 17, 1864; Harrison Diary, August 17, September 3, 1864; Mrs. Hugh Lee Diary, August 20 and 23, 1864.

33. *O.R.* 43, pt. 1, 554–56; Gary Gallagher, *Stephen Dodson Ramseur: Lee's Gallant General* (Chapel Hill: University of North Carolina Press, 1985), 140–44; Robert Thruston Hubard Notebook, Special Collections, Alderman Library, University of Virginia, Charlottesville, Virginia.

34. Freeman, *Lee's Lieutenants*, vol. 3, 601–4; Catton, *Grant Takes Command*, 377–80.

35. *O.R.* 42, pt. 2, 1195–99; ibid. series IV, vol. 3, 379; Ruffin, "A Chapter in Confederate History," 108; Seth Barton French to Colonel Northrop, September 15, 1864, Ruffin Papers.

36. Harrison Diary, August 17, 1864; Pitman Diary, numerous entries for June, July, and August 1864; McKown Diary, numerous entries for June, July, and August 1864; Chase Diary, July 17 and 23, 1864; M. B. Buck to Dear Richard, July 6 and 24, 1864, Richard B. Buck Collection; Laura Lee Diary, July 23, 1864; *Lexington Gazette*, August 2, 1864.

37. *O.R.* 43, pt. 1, 783, 792.

38. Ibid., pt. 139, 156–57, 163, 177, 209–10.

39. Ibid., pt. 2, 209–10, 249.

40. Ibid., pt. 1, 37.

41. Ibid., 429–30, 491, 519; Wilson, *Under the Old Flag*, vol. 1, 560–63.

42. *O.R.* 43, pt. 1, 441–42, 459–60, 463, 467–77, 508–9; ibid. 43, pt. 2, 220.

43. Jedediah Hotchkiss to My Dear Brother, October 3, 1864, Hotchkiss Papers; *O.R.* 43, pt. 2, 249.

44. *O.R.* 43, pt. 1, 720; ibid. 43, pt. 2, 177, 209–10, 253, 293.

45. Ibid., 43, pt. 2, 115, 124–25, 138–39, 148, 159, 167–69, 174–75, 183, 189, 249–50, 253, 258–59, 263, 270, 277, 293.

46. Ibid., 509; ibid. 43, pt. 1, 309.

47. Ibid., 43, pt. 1, 37, 50; ibid. 43, pt. 2, 307–8, 339.

48. Ibid., 43, pt. 1, 477, 529.

49. Ibid., 477, 491; ibid. 43, pt. 2, 288–89, 292, 297.

50. Wesley Merritt, "Sheridan in the Shenandoah Valley," in *Battles and Leaders of the Civil War*, edited by Robert U. Johnson and Clarence B. Buel (reprint, New York: Thomas Yoseloff, 1956), vol. 4, 513; Stephen Z. Starr, *The Union Cavalry in the Civil War* (Baton Rouge: Louisiana State University Press, 1981), vol. 2, 303.

51. Starr, *The Union Cavalry in the Civil War*, vol. 2, 302; James H. Kidd, *Personal Recollections of a Cavalryman* (reprint, Alexandria, Va.: Time-Life Books, 1983), 398–99.

52. Hannaford quoted in Starr, *The Union Cavalry in the Civil War*, vol. 2, 302.

53. Mrs. Hugh Lee Diary, October 16, 1864; Daniel Miller to John T. Harris, December 16, 1864, Harris Papers, Placed on deposit by the Harrisonburg-Rockingham County Historical Society; Jed. Hotchkiss to his brother, October 3, 1864, Hotchkiss Papers; Jno. P. Dull to Dear Giney, November 9, 1864, John Paul Dull Papers, The University Library, Washington and Lee University, Lexington, Virginia; A. C. R. Jones to unaddressed, November 30, 1864, Ann Cary Randolph Jones Family Papers; M. B. Buck to My Dear Richard, November 5, 1864, Richard B. Buck Collection; J. M. Schreckhire to Dear Brother, October 17, 1864, Schreckhire Papers.

54. Jno. P. Dull to Dear Giney, November 9, 1864, Dull Papers; Diary of Creed Thomas Davis, November 30, 1864, Virginia Historical Society, Richmond, Virginia.

55. *O.R.* 43, pt. 2, 308; Wert, *From Winchester to Cedar Creek*, 159; J. M. Schreckhire to Dear Brother, October 17, 1864, Schreckhire Papers.

56. Laura Lee Diary, December 19, 1864; Mrs. Hugh Lee Diary, December 22, 1864.

EPILOGUE

1. Wert, *From Winchester to Cedar Creek*, 250.
2. M. B. Buck to My Dear Richard, January 25, 1865, Richard B. Buck Collection; Hannaford quoted in Stephen Z. Starr, "Winter Quarters Near Winchester, 1864–1865," *Virginia Magazine of History and Biography*, 86 (1978), 329–30.
3. McDonald Diary, 245–47, 251, 254.
4. Daniel Miller to John T. Harris, December 16, 1864; Petitions of Issac Harman, November 29, 1864, James L. Hooke, December 6, 1864, Abraham Knopp, December 10, 1864, William S. Downs, December 1864, Moses Mason, January 4, 1865, Harris Papers, placed on deposit by the Harrisonburg-Rockingham County Historical Society; R. G. Logan to Dear Sir, November 24, 1864, Davidson Papers, WSHS.
5. McDonald Diary, 252, 259.
6. Catton, *Grant Takes Command*, 425–27.
7. McDonald Diary, 247–48; McFarland Diary, January 1, February 3, 1865; Buck Diary, April 5, 1865.
8. McFarland Diary, April 11, 1865; Buck Diary, April 13 and 14, 1865; Preston Diary, April 10, 1865; White Diary, 197–98.

BIBLIOGRAPHY

MANUSCRIPTS
Duke University, Durham, North Carolina
William B. Abbott Papers
Charles Wesley Andrews Papers
Bedinger-Dandridge Family Papers
Alexander Robinson Boteler Papers
Jacob B. Click Papers
James D. Davidson Papers
William Foster Diary
Andrew Funkhouser Papers
Haywood and W. D. Hardy Papers
Wells J. Hawks Papers
Cornelius Hite, Jr. Papers
Frederick William Mackey Holliday Papers
Hooke Papers
Jackson-Trout Papers
Marshall McDonald Papers
James M. Schreckhire Papers
Francis Henny Smith Letters
William Sperow Papers
William G. Thompson Papers
William Weaver Papers
1863 Tax-in-Kind Estimates for Albemarle County, Amherst County, Buckingham County, Fluvanna County, and Nelson County, Virginia

The Handley Library, Winchester, Virginia
Portia Baldwin Baker Diary
Journal of Rev. B. F. Brooke
Julia Chase Diary
Journal of John Peyton Clarke
Harriet H. Griffith Diary
Ann Cary Randolph Jones Papers
Mrs. Hugh Lee Diary
Treadwell Smith Diary
Williams Family Correspondence

James Madison University, Harrisonburg, Virginia
Margaret B. Burress Collection
John T. Harris Papers

Library of Congress, Washington, D.C.
C.S.A. War Department, Report of the Tax-in-Kind
Jedediah Hotchkiss Papers
Mercer Green Johnston Papers
Josephine Forney Roedel Diary

Rockbridge Historical Society, Lexington, Virginia
Confederate States of America Letterbook, 1864–65
James B. Dorman Papers
James Kerr Edmonson Correspondence
William Hale Houston Papers
Morrison Family Papers
Mary Louisa Reid-White Papers

Southern Historical Collection,
University of North Carolina, Chapel Hill
William Patterson Diary
William Nelson Pendleton Papers

Virginia Historical Society, Richmond, Virginia
Robert Y. Conrad Papers
Creed Thomas Davis Diary

Fontaine W. Mahood Papers
Francis Gilbert Ruffin Papers
Alexander H. H. Stuart Papers
Richard Henry Watkins Letters

University of Virginia, Charlottesville, Virginia
Richard Bayly Buck Transcripts
Richard Bayly Buck Collection
Nancy Emerson Diary
Matthella Page Harrison Diary
Robert Thruston Hubard Notebook
Frank Imboden Collection
McCue Family Papers
Francis McFarland Collection
McGuffin Family Papers
Levi Pitman Papers
Alexander H. H. Stuart Papers
Ambrose Timberlake Papers

Washington and Lee University, Lexington, Virginia
Alexander T. Barclay Papers
James D. Davidson Papers
John Paul Dull Papers
Frank Smith Reader Diary

West Virginia University, Morgantown, West Virginia
Jacob M. Campbell Papers
Diary of Sarah Morgan McKown
Diary of a Southern Sympathizer
Waitman T. Willey Papers

College of William and Mary, Williamsburg, Virginia
Laura Lee Diary

Wisconsin State Historical Society, Madison, Wisconsin
James D. Davidson Papers

GOVERNMENT PUBLICATIONS

United States Government. *The Seventh Census of the United States.* Washington, D.C., 1854.

United States Government. *The Eighth Census of the United States.* Washington, D.C., 1864.

United States War Department. *War of the Rebellion: Official Records of the Union and Confederate Armies.* 128 volumes. Washington, D.C., 1880–1901.

NEWSPAPERS

Charlestown Spirit of Jefferson
Charlestown Virginia Free Press
Harrisonburg Valley Democrat
Lexington Gazette
Richmond Dispatch
Richmond Whig
Rockingham Register
Staunton Spectator
Staunton Vindicator
Winchester Republican
Winchester Virginian

BOOKS

Allan, Elizabeth Preston. *The Life and Times of Margaret Junkin Preston.* Boston, 1903.

Ashby, Thomas A. *The Valley Campaigns.* New York, 1914.

Barry, Joseph. *The Annals of Harpers Ferry.* Martinsburg, W. Va., 1872.

Basler, Roy P., ed., *The Collected Works of Abraham Lincoln.* New Brunswick, N.J., 1953.

Baylor, George. *Bull Run to Bull Run.* Richmond, Va., 1900.

Boley, Henry. *Lexington in Old Virginia,* Lexington, Va., 1974.

Boney, F. N. *John Letcher of Virginia.* Tuscaloosa, Ala., 1966.

Buck, Lucy Rebecca. *Sad Earth, Sweet Heaven: The Diary of Lucy Rebecca Buck During the War Between the States, Front Royal, Virginia, December 25, 1861–April 15, 1865.* Edited by William P. Buck, Birmingham, Ala., 1973.

Burnham, W. Dean. *Presidential Ballots, 1836–1892.* Baltimore, 1955.

Bushong, Millard Kessler. *Historic Jefferson County.* Boyce, Va., 1972.

Cartmell, T. K. *Shenandoah Valley Pioneers and Their Descendants*. Berryville, Va., 1963.

Catton, Bruce. *The Coming Fury*. New York, 1961.

——. *Grant Takes Command*. Boston, 1968.

——. *Never Call Retreat*. New York, 1965.

——. *A Stillness at Appomattox*. New York, 1953.

——. *Terrible Swift Sword*. New York, 1963.

Chamberlayne, C. G., ed. *Ham Chamberlayne—Virginian: Letters and Papers of an Artillery Officer in the War for Southern Independence, 1861–1865*. Richmond, Va., 1932.

Davis, William C. *Jefferson Davis: The Man and His Hour*. New York, 1991.

Doherty, William T. *Berkeley County, U.S.A.* Parsons, W.Va., 1972.

Dumond, Dwight Lowell. *The Secession Movement, 1860–1861*. New York, 1931.

Escott, Paul. *After Secession: Jefferson Davis and the Failure of Confederate Nationalism*. Baton Rouge, 1978.

Evans, Willis F. *History of Berkeley County, West Virginia*. Martinsburg, W.Va., 1927.

Faust, Albert B. *The German Element in the United States*. New York, 1927.

Foote, Shelby. *The Civil War: A Narrative*. 3 vols. New York, 1958–74.

Freeman, Douglas Southall, *Lee's Lieutenants: A Study in Command*. 3 vols. New York, 1942–44.

——. *R. E. Lee: A Biography*. 4 vols. New York, 1934.

Gallagher, Gary W. *Stephen Dodson Ramseur: Lee's Gallant General*. Chapel Hill, N.C., 1985.

Goff, Richard. *Confederate Supply*. Durham, N.C., 1969.

Gold, Thomas D. *History of Clarke County, Virginia*. Berryville, Va., 1914.

Gottmann, Jean. *Virginia at Mid-Century*. New York, 1955.

Grant, Ulysses S. *Personal Memoirs of U. S. Grant*. 2 vols. New York, 1885.

Hart, Freeman H. *The Valley of Virginia in the American Revolution, 1763–1789*. Chapel Hill, N.C., 1942.

Harwell, Richard. *Washington*. New York, 1968.

Jennings, Francis. *Empire of Fortune: Crowns, Colonies, and Tribes in the Seven Years War in America*. New York, 1988.

Johannson, Robert W. *Stephen A. Douglas*. New York, 1973.

Johnston, II, Angus James. *Virginia Railroads in the Civil War*. Chapel Hill, N.C., 1961.

Kean, Robert Garlick Hill. *Inside the Confederate Government: The Diary of Robert Garlick Hill Kean*. Edited by Edward Younger. New York, 1957.

Kercheval, Samuel. *A History of the Valley of Virginia*. Woodstock, Va., 1902.

Kidd, J. H. *Personal Recollections of a Cavalryman*. Reprint, Alexandria, Va., 1983.

Leyburn, James G. *The Scotch-Irish: Social History*. Chapel Hill, N.C., 1962.

McDonald, Cornelia. *A Diary with Reminiscences of the War and Refugee Life in the Shenandoah Valley, 1860–1865*. Nashville, Tenn., 1934.

McDonald, William N. *A History of the Laurel Brigade*. Edited by Bushrod C. Washington. Baltimore, 1907.

McGregor, James C. *The Disruption of Virginia*. New York, 1942.

McMurry, Richard M. *Two Great Rebel Armies*. Chapel Hill, N.C., 1989.

McPherson, James M. *Battle Cry of Freedom: The Civil War Era*. New York, 1988.

———. *Ordeal by Fire: The Civil War and Reconstruction*. New York, 1982.

Moore, Edward A. *The Story of a Cannoneer Under Stonewall Jackson*. Reprint, Alexandria, Va., 1981.

Morton, Frederick. *The Story of Winchester in Virginia*. Strasburg, Va., 1925.

Morton, Oren F. *A History of Rockbridge County, Virginia*. Staunton, Va., 1920.

Morton, Richard L. *Colonial Virginia. Volume Two: Westward Expansion and Prelude to Revolution 1710–1763*. Chapel Hill, N.C., 1960.

Nevins, Allan. *The Emergence of Lincoln. Volume Two: Prologue to Civil War*. New York, 1950.

Paxton, Frank. *The Civil War Letters of General Frank "Bull" Paxton, C.S.A.* Edited by John G. Paxton, Hillsboro, Tex., 1978.

Peyton, J. Lewis. *History of Augusta County, Virginia*. Reprint, Bridgewater, Va., 1953.

Potter, David. *The Impending Crisis*. New York, 1976.

Quarles, Garland R. *Occupied Winchester, 1861–1865*. Winchester, Va., 1976.

Shanks, Henry T. *The Secession Movement in Virginia, 1847–1861*. Richmond, 1934.

Sheridan, Philip H. *Personal Memoirs of P. H. Sheridan*. 2 vols. New York, 1888.

Starr, Stephen Z. *The Union Cavalry in the Civil War*. 3 vols. Baton Rouge, 1978–85.

Stevens, George T. *Three Years in the Sixth Corps*. Reprint, Alexandria, Va., 1984.

Strickler, Harry M. *A Short History of Page County, Virginia*. Richmond, Va., 1952.

Summers, Festus P. *The Baltimore and Ohio Railroad in the Civil War*. New York, 1939.

Tanner, Robert G. *Stonewall in the Valley: Thomas J. "Stonewall" Jackson's Shenandoah Valley Campaign, Spring 1862*. New York, 1976.

Turner, Charles W., editor. *Old Zeus: Life and Letters (1860–1862) of James J. White*. Verona, Va., 1983.

Turner, George E. *Victory Rode the Rails*. New York, 1953.

Van Deusen, Glyndon G. *William Henry Seward*. New York, 1967.

Waddell, Joseph A. *Annals of Augusta County, Virginia, from 1726–1871*. Reprint, Harrisonburg, Va., 1979.

Wayland, John W. *A History of Shenandoah County, Virginia*. Strasburg, Va., 1927.

———. *The German Element of the Shenandoah Valley of Virginia*. Reprint, Bridgewater, Va., 1964.

Wert, Jeffry D. *From Winchester to Cedar Creek: The Shenandoah Campaign of 1864*. Carlisle, Pa., 1987.

White, Rev. William S. *Rev. William S. White, D.D. and His Times: An Autobiography*. Richmond, Va., 1891.

Wilson, Howard McKnight. *Great Valley Patriots*. Verona, Va., 1976.

Wilson, James Harrison. *Under the Old Flag*. 2 vols. Reprint, Westport, Ct., 1971.

Wilson, William L. *A Borderline Confederate*. Edited by Festus P. Summers. Pittsburgh, Pa., 1962.

Wooster, Ralph A. *The Secession Conventions of the South*. Princeton, N.J., 1962.

ARTICLES AND DISSERTATIONS

Felt, Jeremy P. "Lucius B. Northrop and the Confederacy's Subsistence Department." *Virginia Magazine of History and Biography* 69 (April 1961).

Greenwalt, Bruce S. "Life Behind Confederate Lines in Virginia: The Correspondence of James D. Davidson." *Civil War History* 16 (September 1970).

———. "Unionists in Rockbridge County: The Correspondence of James Dorman Davidson Concerning the Virginia Secession Convention of 1861." *Virginia Magazine of History and Biography* 73 (January 1965).

Hay, Thomas R. "Lucius B. Northrop: Commissary General of the Confederacy." *Civil War History* 9 (March 1963).

Hershberger, Guy F. "Mennonites in the Civil War." *The Mennonite Quarterly Review* 18 (Fall 1948).

Imboden, John D. "Jackson at Harper's Ferry in 1861." In *Battles and Leaders of the Civil War*, vol. 1, edited by Robert U. Johnson and Clarence Clough Buel. New York, 1956.

———. "The Confederate Retreat from Gettysburg." In *Battles and Leaders of the Civil War*, vol. 3, edited by Robert U. Johnson and Clarence Clough Buel. New York, 1956.

Merritt, Wesley. "Sheridan in the Shenandoah Valley." In *Battles and Leaders of the Civil War,* vol. 4, edited by Robert U. Johnson and Clarence Clough Buel. New York, 1956.

Montague, Ludwell Lee. "Subsistence of the Army of the Valley." *Military Affairs* 12 (Winter 1948).

Phillips, Edward H. "The Lower Shenandoah Valley during the Civil War: The Impact of War upon the Civilian Population and upon Civil Institutions." Ph.D. dissertation, University of North Carolina, 1958.

Ramsdell, Charles W. "The Confederate Government and the Railroads." *American Historical Review* 22 (July 1917).

―――. "General Robert E. Lee's Horse Supply, 1862–1865." *American Historical Review* 35 (July 1930).

Riggs, David F. "Robert Young Conrad and the Ordeal of Secession." *Virginia Magazine of History and Biography* 86 (July 1978).

Ruffin, Francis Gilbert. "A Chapter in Confederate History." *North American Review* 30 (July 1882).

Schlebecker, John T. "Farmers in the Lower Shenandoah Valley, 1850." *Virginia Magazine of History and Biography* 79 (October 1971).

Snapp, George H. "The Civil War Diary of George Snapp." Transcription by Roger E. Sappinton. *Rockingham Recorder* 3 (April 1985).

Starr, Stephen Z. "Winter Quarters Near Winchester, 1864–1865." *Virginia Magazine of History and Biography* 86 (July 1978).

Turner, Charles W. "The Virginia Central Railroad at War, 1861–1865." *The Journal of Southern History* 20 (April 1942).

Wayland, John W. "Early German Settlement of the Shenandoah Valley." *Virginia Magazine of History and Biography* 9 (April 1909).

INDEX